Dedicated to all the brave men of Pershore
who served their King & Country
during the Great War of 1914-1918

Remembering with Honour
Those that Fell.

Pershore Men
of the Great War

A continuation of the research carried out by
Malcolm Farmer of Cornmore, Pershore

With acknowledgements and grateful thanks to:

Derek Farmer for all his sincere kindness in supporting this project and
allowing us to develop Malcolm's work to bring about this
commemorative book

Newsquest Media Group Ltd for allowing us to print archived reports
from the Evesham Journal & Worcester Berrow's Journal
http://www.eveshamjournal.co.uk/

Commonwealth War Graves Commission for granting permission to
print the various Certificates and information
http://www.cwgc.org/

Sandra Taylor from "Remember the Fallen" for all her help, information,
friendship & support
http://www.rememberthefallen.co.uk/

The family of the late Marshall Wilson, Ernie Fuller, Kevin Fuller,
Michael Turvey and various Pershore families for assisting this project
with their local knowledge and memorabilia. Especially to the members
of the 2014 Facebook Group "Memories of Pershore's Past"
https://www.facebook.com/groups/531821243592643/

To Wychavon District Council for allocating a grant of £250
to this project
http://www.wychavon.gov.uk/

ISBN: 978-1-909219-22-9

Index

A Tribute to Malcolm Farmer

10th December 1953 – 22nd February 2013

Malcolm Farmer was born on 10th December 1953 and lived in Mayfield Road in Pershore. He was a very clever chap and was always reading – often several books at one time. He attended Prince Henry's Grammar School and then Warwick University to study Chemistry. He was very reserved and lived a simplistic life at his house in Cornmore with his cats and beloved books. He contributed to at least one book and was prolific in submitting citations for the Science Fiction Citations website related to first recorded use of phrases in Science Fiction novels.

In the 1980's, Malcolm carried out a lot of research into his family history. This sparked creation of websites for adding to the national record of War Memorial inscriptions, scanning and placing on-line scans of old Maps of Worcestershire and surrounding counties and the production of a paper containing obituaries and photos of Pershore Men who Died in the Great War. He was constantly updating this document, even doing so the week before he died.

He has contributed to Project Gutenberg by digitalising a number of obscure out of print and out of copyright books. He has done the same with many issues of Punch. So that he could conserve some of his old books he attended classes to learn bookbinding.

Malcolm died suddenly but peacefully on 22nd February 2013 aged 59 and his files went to his brother Derek. Thanks to articles in the local newspapers, Derek learned via a friend of our project to create this Centenary Memorial to the men of Pershore who served during the First World War. He made contact with me and kindly shared all

Malcolm's files and research. This included many of the press quotations which he had painstakingly obtained over many years from the Microfiche archive files of the local newspapers in the Library.

Paying tribute to Malcolm, Derek said "Malcolm was many things to many people - he was your friend at University, he was your housemate, he was your colleague at QE medical centre in Birmingham, he was your drinking buddy, he was your friend, he was your neighbour, he was your colleague at Prince Henry's , he was your nephew, he was your cousin, he was your partner, he was your brother in law, he was my brother - he will not be forgotten".

Thanks to the wealth of information now also available online, I have spent the last 6 months painstakingly adding to this information, filling in more of the gaps, re-typing and editing to bring you this book today. I hope to continue researching and any further information I find will be uploaded to the Centenary Memorial Website at http://pershoreww1.webs.com and on the Facebook page https://www.facebook.com/pershoreww1

Please bear in mind that it is often difficult to research the survivors as most of the service records of WW1 military personnel were destroyed during the bombing in WW2. Those that died tend to have an article in the local newspapers and they are recorded in several places. If there is anybody who has been missed off, please accept our sincere apologies and know that this is simply because we have found no record of their service. We have endeavoured to be as accurate as we can with the information available with the sole intention of producing a long-standing memorial to all those brave men from our town who fought for King and Country. Each year, the Fallen are remembered during the Remembrance Service in Pershore Abbey where their names are read out. We hope that this provides some background to the men behind those names and that they, as well as those who survived the war and had to live with the consequences afterwards, remain in our thoughts and hearts forever more.

Mrs Trudy Burge

Hon Secretary - Pershore & District Royal Naval Association

Private Charles Frederick ANDREWS
Service No: 240111
Age: 28
Of the 1st/8th Worcestershire Regiment
Died in France on 9th Oct 1917. Killed in Action.
Went out on 8th October 1917. Buried in Dochy Farm
New British Cemetery, Belgium.
Son of James & Eliza Andrews of Head Street,
Pershore.

Trooper James Oswald ANDREWS
Service No: 3025
Age:23
Of the Queen's Own Worcestershire Hussars. Worc
Regiment. Died of wounds in Egypt on 28th April 1913.
First wounded 23rd April 1916. Buried in Kantara War
Memorial Cemetery, Egypt. 1st Draft, embarked at
Devonport 23rd October 1915 for service with the
Mediterranean Expeditionary Force, disembarked at
Mudros 6th November 1915, disembarked at Alexandria,
Egypt on 30th November 1915.
Listed in the Evesham Journal 20th May 1916 as having died of
wounds.
Son of James & Eliza Andrews of Head Street, Pershore.
Brother of Charles Frederick, Frank and George Sidney.

Private Reginald Francis ANDREWS
Service No 3425
Age: 20
Of the 1st/8th Battalion Worcestershire Regiment
(Queen's Own Worcestershire Hussars)
Killed in action at Flanders on 20th July 1916
Buried in Bapaume Post Military Cemetery,
Albert, France, Grave I. F. 7.
Enlisted at Worcester.
Lived in Tewkesbury, Gloucestershire
Listed as a Servant at Allesborough Farm on the 1911 Census.

Private James Samuel ANNIS
Service No: 43703
Age: 23

10th Battalion Lincolnshire Regiment. Formerly
Service No: 4657 of 3rd/8th Worcs Regiment. Enlisted
In Pershore under the "Derby" scheme of December
1915 and called up early 1916. Killed in action in
France on 28th April 1917. Commemorated on Arras
Memorial, France, Bay 3 and 4.
Son of Charles and Miriam Annis, of Pensham,
Pershore formerly of Binholme, Pershore

Pte. J. Annis, C
Pershore. Killed. B

<u>Evesham Journal 4 June 1917</u> - COUSINS KILLED.

*A letter from a Pershore man, Lance-Corpl. John Gould, Royal
Engineers, announced the death in a recent action of two cousins, Pte.
James Annis, son of Mr. and Mrs. Annis, of Pensham, and Sapper
Edward John Marshall, son of Mr. and Mrs. Charles Marshall, of the
Newlands, Pershore, both of the Lincolns. The sad news has since
been officially confirmed, and thus two more names are added to
Pershore's Roll of Honour. Pte. Annis was 23 years of age, and his
cousin 24. Both joined up under the group system, and were
transferred from the Worcesters to the Lincolns. Both families have the
sympathies of the Townspeople in their sad loss. In a letter to Mrs.
Annis, the lieutenant of the company says to Mrs Annis, her son was a
good soldier, who did his duty fearlessly, faithfully, and well. Sapper
Marshall's brother Philip, who was badly gassed in action last January,
is now a substitute working on the land at Evesham."*

**Excerpt from 10th Battalion Lincolnshire Regt (Grimsby Chums) diaries printed with the
kind permission of Ian Jackson:**

1917 – <u>Arras</u>

*The Chums, now part of the Third Army, were not the same fighting
force they were in 1916. Their ranks of Grimsby men had been diluted
by new drafts. They were now to attack in the Arras sector in support of
the diversion for the French Army attack on the Aisne. A small
bombardment of four days was arranged for this battle. It was 9th April
1917.*

The first wave set off at 5.30 am with great success. The enemy lines were reached and occupied. A creeping barrage then allowed the Chums to make further attacks,1500 yards forward of their start positions. This attack was no repeat of the Somme, and although there were casualties, the objectives were reached and the Chums could "dig in" on captured territory. The Chums were now on the forward slopes Vimy Ridge, and were able to look down on the enemy across the Doui plain in front of them. The Chums had played their part in the most successful day of the war so far. After a brief period of rest out of the line, the Lincolns carried on with the offensive. The target was not an open countryside target of the previous week, but a heavily fortified town position at Reoux, and it's Chemical Works. The Chums Brigade were to attack on April 28th. The attack was started at 4.15 am but was not destined to be a success. Forming up in the open alerted the Germans who opened up with mortar and machine guns. The Chums set off already fragmented. The attack was soon broken up, with small groups of isolated men unable to continue. A German counter attack at 8.00 am led to a retreat and was effectively the end of the Chums attack. The losses were high, 420 dead, missing and wounded. The Battalion was withdrawn from the line on 30th April, shattered.

Private James ARCHER
Service No: 2430
Age: 20
6th Battalion Welsh Regiment. Died from wounds on
16th March 1916. Buried in Bethune Town Cemetery,
France
Son of Joseph & Ellen Archer. Born in
Birmingham, lived in Newlands in Pershore.

Evesham Journal 1st Apr 1916

"Pte James Archer of the Welsh Regt. Son of Mr & Mrs Archer of the Newlands, Pershore died in hospital on March 16 from shell wounds. The Chaplain of the Regt communicated the sad news to the family and a chum of deceased states in a letter:- "We were resting in a village about 4 miles from the trenches when the enemy sent in a few shells unexpectedly. Jim was hit just as he was fetching his dinner". Pte Archer was a native of Pershore and prior to the war was a miner in

Wales. Joined the Army in Sept 1914 and had been at the front for a year without leave

Private William ASKEW
Service No: 5487
Age: 17
2nd/20th Battalion London Regiment. Killed in action on 15th August 1916. Buried on Ecoivres Military Cemetery, Mont-St. Eloi, France, Grave III. D. 25.
Son of Alfred Rigby Askew and Elizabeth Askew of Newlands, Pershore.

William Askew

Evesham Journal 9th September 1916 "PERSHORE LAD KILLED.*

News has been received from the War Office that Pte William Askew, son of Mr & Mrs A R Askew, late of Pershore, has been killed in action on August 15th last. The deceased lad was a native of Pershore, was well known and respected in his native town. He was until quite recently a scholar of the Baptist Sunday School.

He left Pershore in July 1914 for Birmingham and was employed at the British Insulated and Helsby Cable Co. in Livery Street until the time of his enlistment in the R.A.M.C. He joined at the age of 16 and was transferred to the 20th County of the London Regt in May 1916. Was sent to France at the end of June. He, with several others, was blown up by a trench mine. His Captain, writing to his parents spoke of the lad's pluck and of the great attachment that existed between them."

Private John BAGNALL
Service No: 3149
Age: 23
Queen's Own Worcestershire Hussars (Worcester Yeomanry) Killed in action on 23rd April 1916 in Egypt Commemorated on Jerusalem Memorial, Israel, Panel 3 & 5.
Son of Clara Thorneycroft (formerly Bagnall), 34 Cannock Rd., Fallings Park, Wolverhampton and the late Edward Bagnall.
Evesham Journal, 25 June 1915:-- FROM MISSION HALL TO KHAKI.

"One of the latest recruits from Pershore, which town has done so well in the shedding of civilian frees for the khaki uniform, is Captain John Bagnall, of the Church Army Mission, who has joined the Worcestershire Yeomanry. The captain will preach his farewell session at the Mission Hall, Pershore, next Sunday evening, and then will immediately leave to commence his military training. His loss will be severely felt by a host of friends who have been associated with him in the work of the mission, of which he took charge nearly two years ago. While the Captain's decision has occasioned much surprise -- his gentle demeanour seeming quite incompatible with the choice of a military life -- his intimate friends knew how deeply he was convinced of the justice."

Evesham Journal 26th August 1916 "THE YEOMANRY"

Welcome news has been received of the safety of many officers and men of the Worcestershire Yeomanry who in the first instance were supposed to have been killed in the surprise engagement with the Turks at Katia on Easter Sunday but the prolonged silence as to the fate of Capt. Bagnall, formerly of Pershore, is regarded by his .friends with the gravest apprehension. Capt Bagnall was a Church Army Worker in connection with the Church of England and the influence of his earnest, self-denying labours in the district will long remain. With his delicate physique and pale and thoughtful cast of countenance, it is impossible to say that Captain Bagnall had the appearance of a fighting man but he was dominated with the thought that for England, this was a righteous conflict and saw clearly involved the principles of liberty and right when he resigned his work at Pershore for the stern duty of war."

Driver John BARBER
Service No 831055
Age:34
"C" Battery 241st Brigade Royal Artillery
Died in Pershore on 21st July 1919 of war-related
sickness. Buried in Pershore Cemetery. Serving in
Italy in early 1918. CWGC grave in Pershore cemetery.
His original service number was 3067 Originally posted to the Battery
Ammunition Column (this was based pre-war in Malvern). Transferred

from BAC to 2nd Section Divisional Ammunition Column 15/5/16. Date of transfer to C/241 (Redditch battery) not known.
Husband of Annie Alice Barber(nee Salmon) of 7 Bearcroft Cottages, Pershore.

Private William Robert BARBER
Service No 203746
Age:32

"B" Company 1st/7th Battalion Worcs Regiment
Killed in action at Flanders France on 16th August 1917.
Commemorated on Tyne Cot Memorial, Belgium, Panel
75 to 77. Memorial on his parent's grave at Pershore
Son of William & Rhoda Barber of Priest Lane, Pershore.

<u>Evesham Journal 15 September 1917</u>

``Mr. W. Barber, of Priest-lane, has received a letter from Capt. Percy Carter (who now lies badly wounded) that his son, Pte. William Barber, was killed on the 16th ult. After assuring the bereaved parents of his deep sympathy, the captain states that Will was reported missing after a night attack, but his body was discovered some time afterwards. He gave his life while gallantly doing his duty. Pte. Barber had been out in France eighteen months, during which time he was twice wounded and gassed. Before joining the colours, he worked as a painter and decorator for Mr. A. Salisbury, of Evesham. He was engaged to be married."*

Private Oliver Henry BARNES
Service No 12310
Age: 23

4th Battalion Worcs Regiment. Killed in action in
Gallipoli on 6th August 1915. Commemorated on Helles
Memorial in Turkey, Panel 104 to 113. Born Pinvin;
enlisted at Worcester (living at Pinvin when he enlisted)
Brother of Mrs. Clara Davies, 14 Council Cottages, Pinvin
Sister married Leonard Preece of Little Priest Lane.

Private Harry James BEARD
Service No 64245
Age: 19
1st Battalion West Yorkshire Regiment (Prince of Wales's
Own) Killed in action at Flanders France on 24th
September 1918. Buried in Trefcon British Cemetery,
Caulaincourt, France, Grave C. 26
Son of Harry & Alice Beard of Newlands, Pershore

Harry James Beard

Sergeant Arthur BIDDULPH
Service No 3914
Age: 38
4th Battalion Worcestershire Regiment. Killed in action
On 4th June 1915 in Gallipoli. Commemorated on Helles
Memorial, Turkey, Panel 104 to 113.
Father of Grace I. Biddulph, 129 Leonard Rd.,
Handsworth, Birmingham

Arthur Biddulph

Evesham Journal 31st July 1915 – "PERSHORE MAN KILLED"

*"Sergt. Arthur Biddulph, a representative as worth as any of The
Gallant 4th Worcesters, was killed on 4th June when fighting in the
Gallipoli Peninsula. Mrs Biddulph of Pershore, who now lives with her
Mother Mrs Jones of Priest Lane, received the official intimation of his
death on Tuesday. She had heard previously from the authorities that
he was missing and had entertained little hope of ever seeing him
again since receiving the verbal message from another Pershore
soldier who came back wounded from the Dardanelles at the beginning
of the month that he himself saw the Sergt. struck down by a bullet.*

*This soldier, Pte. William Reeves but 20 years of age, was sent out
after 4 month's training and received his baptism of fire in the very fight
in which Sergt. Biddulph was killed. It happened in the afternoon of
that June day; they had taken four trenches from the Turks and were
about to rush the fifth and the Sergeant came to him, put his hand on
his shoulder and said "Keep close to me lad – you'll be all right". It was
in that rush he saw the sergeant receive his death wound. "I dare not
turn back to see if I could help him" said Pte Reeves. "The orders were
strict that no man was to do this as the Service Corps were following
up to do this work. I rushed on and soon after was shot myself through*

the thigh. The sergeant, Pte Reeves added, was as cool as a cucumber all through, which had a steadying effect on new recruits like himself of whom there were many in this regiment. It was with the greatest reluctance that the boy soldier brought this sad news home to the widowed wife but he thought it was his duty to say what he actually saw.

One feels all the more admiration for the brave sergeant on hearing of how he tried to cheer up his young companion. He was an experienced soldier; had served over his time – 22 years – and had been right through the South Africa campaign. He was a tall, fine looking soldier, quiet, reserved, wonderfully efficient in all his military duties, well-liked by the men and valued by his superior officers. He was at Croome training with his regiment when war broke out and was at once despatched to Plymouth, where he worked almost night and day drilling and instructing troops. He went to several other places doing similar work and about Christmas was quite run down in health. Instead of going to hospital, he came home and while in Pershore saw Dr Emerson who told him he needed to take rest. He was too good a soldier, however, to take rest while such a war was going on and in a few days he returned to his duties. For a short time he was at Norton Barracks drilling recruits there and on occasions when at Pershore he gave instruction to the Volunteer Training Corps in Swedish drill and there is not a member of that body who was not favourably impressed by his quiet efficiency and soldier-like qualities. Sergt. Biddulph leaves a wife and three children, one of whom was born in India.

A MILITARY FAMILY. On a representative of the Journal calling on Mrs Biddulph to gain some particulars of the sergeant and request the loan of his photograph, he was surprised to learn the extent of the family's interest in the war. The walls of the cottage are covered with portraits of soldiers. Her Father 'Ensor' Jones, who has been thirty years connected with the Army, is now acting as a reservist in Banbury; her Brother, Sergt. Jack Jones, was badly wounded in the fight at Neuve Chapelle – he is a Worcester man and has five Brothers now serving in the trenches and two on garrison duty; her Sister's Fiancé Pte. Lionel Thomas, a young South African, was killed at Neuve Chapelle and the daily lament of her youngest Brother, Albert Jones, who is a Lance-Corporal in the Pershore Boy's Brigade, is that he is too young to enlist. While justly proud of the record of their family, there is much sorrow in this little home in Pershore over those who will *never return and a great unceasing anxiety for the safety of others. Sergt. Biddulph's age was 38."*

Private Oliver BIRT
Service No 3329
Age: 38
2nd/8th Battalion Worcestershire Regiment
Died aged 38 on 4th December 1916 at Flanders
Buried in Contay British Cemetery, Contay, France,
Grave VIII. C. 29.
Son of Charles Edward & Eliza Birt of Pershore Fields

Private Arthur Cyril BOZZARD
Service No 325531
Age: 17
Queen's Own Worcestershire Hussars
(Worcester Yeomanry)
Killed in action on 23rd April 1916 in Egypt.
Commemorated on Jerusalem Memorial, Israel, Panel
3 and 5. A.C. Bozzard 1st/1st Worcester Yeomanry,
1st Draft, embarked at Devonport 23rd October 1915 for
service with the Mediterranean Expeditionary Force,
disembarked at Mudros 6th November 1915, disembarked
at Alexandria, Egypt on 30th November 1915. Arthur was
an employee of Messrs. Phillips & Sons in High St.
Son of George & Alice Bozzard of Priest Lane, Pershore

Rifleman Alfred BRANT
Service No 51871
Age: 22
Rifleman in 2nd/8th Battalion West Yorkshire Regiment
(Prince of Wales's Own)
Formerly Service No: 20301, Royal Berkshire Regiment.
Enlisted in Pershore, went out on 20th August 1916.
Killed in action at Flanders on 27th July 1918
Commemorated on Soissons Memorial, France.
Worked at his Father's wood business before joining up.
Son of Edward & Annie Brant of Priest Lane, Pershore

Private William BRIDGEWATER
Service No 18884
Age: 46

1st Battalion Worcestershire Regiment
Killed in action on 4th March 1917 at Flanders.
Born in Milson, Shropshire. Enlisted in Tenbury and went
out in March 1917. Buried in Fins New British Cemetery,
Sorel-Le-Grand, France, Grave VII. C. 19.
Husband of Lily nee Turvey of Head Street, Pershore

Evesham Journal, 12 May 1917 - *ANOTHER PERSHORE MAN KILLED. "Pte. William Bridgewater, of Pershore, who was a sniper in the Worcester Regt. has, it is officially reported, been killed in France. It is but a little more than a year since he married Miss Lily Turvey, of Pershore, who is now left a widow with one child. In a letter of sympathy to Mrs. Bridgewater, Pte. G. Hall, of an E. Lancashire Regt. who was a pal of the deceased, gives a few brief particulars of his death. It appears he was, with four others, in a deep dug out when a large shell dropped close to the entrance, injuring and burying them all. Two managed after a most exhaustive effort to dig their way out and crawled to where Hall was stationed. They said the other two were dead, and Hall writes that he went personally to ascertain if it was correct. It took a long time, he says, to dig down, as the Germans were shelling the ammunition dump just at the back of the trench the unfortunate man was in charge of. He found both were dead, evidently killed by the shock of the explosion. One was Pte. Bridgewater, and the writer forwarded photographs which he found on him. His pocket book and identification disc were handed to the platoon officer. Much sympathy is felt with Mrs. Bridgewater in her bereavement"*

Private Albert R BROOKES
Service No 9671
Age: 19

2nd Battalion Oxford and Bucks Light Infantry
WW1 records show born in Pershore.
Killed in action on 21st October 1914 at Flanders.
Commemorated on Ypres (Menin Gate) Memorial,
Belgium, Panel 37 and 39.

Albert R. Brookes

**Son of Mrs Susan Cosnett, Stepson of Samuel Cosnett
of Top Newlands, Pershore**

Another Pershore young fellow, Private Albert Ralph Brooks, whose portrait we reproduce below has fallen fighting for his country. He was killed in action on October 21. The sad news was communicated to his Mother from the War Office with a brief but poignant letter from Lord Kitchener expressing the "very real sympathy of the King and Queen". Private Brooks, as his photo indicates, was a well set-up young man and though scarcely 20 years of age, had served four years in the Army. As a lad he worked for Mr A W Smith, Chemist of Pershore but his Mother says "A soldier's life for me" was the burden of his talk and the evident great desire of his heart. On presenting himself at the recruiting office he was told he was big enough but not old enough and therefore went back for about eighteen months. He then spent the intervening time in assisting his Step-Father, Mr Sam Cosnett, in making those patent fruit-picking ladders for which he has required a name.

On the expiration of the time waiting, he became a soldier in the King's Own Riffles in the same regiment in which Mr H C Porter of Birlingham was then a Lieutenant. About a year later, he transferred to the Oxfordshire Light Infantry (the old 53rd) of which, singularly enough, another local officer, Col H Davies son of the late General H F Davies of Elmley Castle was commander. In this regiment, in which he died, Private Brooks attained great proficiency in shooting. Some two years ago when General Davies went to see his son, he brought back a message which he straight away delivered to Private Brooks' Mother "that her son during the short time he had been a soldier had gained honours which a man would be proud to have after 20 years' service". This message was delivered by the Rev. Hawkes Field, then master of the Pershore Troop of Boy Scouts to which the young soldier formerly belonged.

Private Brooks won numerous money prizes for good shooting and in 1913 secured possession of the cross guns. His latest success in this all-important feature of military service was the winning of a beautiful silver watch for the championship in Class B. He sent this proud trophy home to his Mother who now possesses it. Private Brooks fought in some of the earliest engagements of the war and while his letters to his Mother were cheerful and encouraging, as it was his kind intention they should be, those to his Aunt Mrs T Brooks of the Newlands revealed he was experiencing tremendous hardships. These letters also display the same spirit actuating the rank and file as of those higher in position and authority, who perhaps realise more deeply the tremendous issues of this universal conflict – that is "the Germans must be crushed and we (the British) shall do our part towards this object". We subscribe our sympathy towards the Mother in the loss of her gallant soldier boy, to whom she was as deeply attached as he was to her.

Private Arthur BUCKLE
Service No 22798
Age: 33
4th Battalion Worcestershire Regiment
Died of wounds on 29th October 1916 in
Birmingham. Born in Pershore, enlisted in
Birmingham. Went to Dardanelles 1915. Came back
discharged. Re-joined and went out to France.
Buried in England, Nunhead (All Saints) Cemetery,
London. Screen Wall. 89. 32539.

Arthur Buckle

**Husband of Florence Elizabeth Buckle of Bull Entry,
Newlands, Pershore. Son of William & Hannah Buckle of
Newlands. 3 of his Brothers also served during WW1.**

Major Bertram James Falkland CARTLAND
Age: 42
1st Battalion Worcestershire Regiment
Killed in action aged 42 at Flanders 27th May 1918
Commemorated on Soissons Memorial, France.
**Husband of Mary Hamilton Cartland of Amerie
Court, Pershore. Father of Dame Mary Barbara
Cartland**

Was a Captain at the outbreak of war and is listed as such in the
1915 Pershore Almanac and Evesham Journal reference. Lived for a while at Amerie Court at the top of Newlands in Pershore. Mentioned in Dispatches 22nd June 1915, 5th May 1916 when he was a Captain, 18th December 1917 when he was a Lt. Col.
There is a memorial to him in the churchyard of Tewkesbury Abbey.
Two of his sons died in WW2 and his wife Mary are also listed on the

memorial. He is listed on the Ashchurch (Glos) war memorial and the Roll of Honour in Worcester Cathedral.

Evesham Journal, 8 June 1918   - *MAJOR CARTLAND KILLED.*

We regret to announce the death of Major J.B.F. Cartland. Mrs. Cartland received the news late on Wednesday evening that Major Cartland had been killed in action on May 27th in the battle of the Aisne. For many years, Major and Mrs. Cartland resided at Amerie Court, Pershore. Major Cartland was widely known in political circles. He was secretary of the Pershore Primrose league Habitation and also Provincial Secretary of the Primrose League for five counties, including Worcestershire and Gloucestershire. He was also private secretary to the member for South Worcestershire, Lieut.Com. B. Eyres Monsell, R.N., M.P.

On the outbreak of war, being in the General Reserve, he was attached to the 5th Batt. Worcesters at Tregantle. He went out to France in November 1914, as A.P.M. on the Staff of the 8th Division under General Davies (now Lieut. Gen. Sir Francis Davies, K.C.B., K.C.M.G., Military Secretary). He held that post for eleven months, returning to England on sick leave, after which he went to Leaford as Garrison Adjutant for eight months.

In November 1916 he went out again to France as Instructor at the G.H.Q. School at St. Omer. That school was done away with in March 1917 and he was attached to the 10th. Batt. Worcesters. He went all through the Messines battles with that battalion, returning to England sick in August, and was in hospital for over a month. He went out again to France in November 1917, to the 3rd Batt. 25th Division, and was all the winter on the Cambrai front. In March of this year he got orders to join another battalion as second in command, and he remained with that battalion till he met his death on May 27.

He was the only son of the late Mr. James Cartland, of Bectis Lodge, Edgbaston. He was born in May, 1876. He was educated at Eastbourne and Charter House, and in 1900 married Mary Hamilton, fourth daughter of the late Col. Scobell, of the Down House, Redmarley, Gloucester, and leaves one daughter and two sons, besides his widow, to mourn his loss.

Major J.B.F. Cartland, Worcestershire Regiment, previously reported killed May 27, then reported missing, is now reported to have been Killed by shell fire on that date. The Act. Capt. Pratt, now a prisoner in Germany, has written to his wife telling her Major Cartland was killed at his side by a shell.

Private Francis A CHARLWOOD
Service No 30291
Age: 31

9th Battalion Worcestershire Regiment
Killed in action on 15th December 1916 in
Mesopotamia. Francis was in 5th and 9th Worcesters.
Joined up 29th May 1916. Buried 2 miles South of Kut.
Commemorated on Basra Memorial, Iraq, Panel 18
and 63.
Son of Joseph & Elizabeth Charlwood of London Bank (Allesborough), Pershore.

Evesham Journal 30th December 1916 – "Official news has just come through that another Pershore man and a popular young fellow, Pte. Francis Charlwood of the New Road has been killed. He leaves a widow (who is in a Birmingham munition factory at present) and two children. He was the son of Mr & Mrs Joseph Charlwood of London Bank Pershore".

Sapper Harry CHARLWOOD
Service No WR/257025
Age: 38

Royal Engineers – joined in 1916.
Died on 23rd October 1918 in Pershore from
Pneumonia In Norwich Military Hospital after serving
abroad. Buried in Pershore Cemetery Grave N.194
Great Western Railway Roll of Honour:
Harry Charlwood Packer/Engineer/Droitwich Sapper
275th Railway Company, Royal Engineers
Son of Joseph & Elizabeth Charlwood, Brother of Fred and Frank of London Bank (Allesborough), Pershore.

Corporal William Frank CHECKETTS
Service No 43100
Age: 25
3rd Royal Berkshire Regiment - formerly No 1514 of
1st/8th Battalion Worcestershire Regiment
Died of war-related sickness aged 25 on 3rd July 1920.
Buried in Pershore Cemetery, Worcestershire, England
Grave J. 16.
Son of Hubert & Ellen Checketts of Head St, Pershore

Private John CLARK(E)
Service No 10213
Age: 35
(Spelt Clarke on Commonwealth War Graves
Commission) Also on Birlingham War Memorial
& St James 'Church) 2nd Battalion Worcs Regiment.
Killed in action at Flanders on 10th March 1915
Enlisted at Worcester. Came from Africa to France 1914.
Commemorated on Le Touret Memorial, France, Panel 17 and 18.
Pershore Abbey War Memorial - surname spelt Clark. Birlingham War
Memorial & St James's Church spelt Clarke. Born and resident
Pershore
Brother of Maudie Playdon
of Engine Terrace in Priest Lane. Son of John & Maltida Clarke
of Pensham.

Evesham Journal 15th March 1915 – ANOTHER PERSHORE
SOLDIER KILLED.

"Private J Clarke of the 1st Worcesters was killed in action on March
10. He was a native of Pershore and the youngest of a family of
twelve. He joined the Army nine years ago prior to which he worked for
the late Mr Thomas Kings of The Chestnuts.

He was re-called from Egypt on the outbreak of war and went straight
into action. He took part in several hot engagements and was
invalided home about Christmas suffering with frost-bitten feet, a
complaint which has affected many of the Worcesters who have been
called upon to bear their full share of the hardship of battling in the
trenches. After a month's furlough, he returned again to France on the

1st inst., and nine days later was killed by a bullet. He was 38 years of age."

Private Albert Austin COLDICOTT
Service No 39717
Age:19
4th Battalion Worcestershire Regiment formerly of
Worcester Yeomanry. Died aged 19, 28th October 1916
at Flanders. Buried in Longueval Road Cemetery,
France, Grave H. 6.
Son of Alfred & Jane Coldicott of Broad St, Pershore

Albert Coldicott

Evesham Journal 25th November 1916 – PTE. COLDICOTT KILLED.

"Pte. Albert Coldicott or 'Cherub' as he was always called in Pershore, was recently killed in action on the battlefield in France and the townspeople generally refer to the event in terms of the deepest regret. He was only a lad of 19 and was as popular in the town as his Father 'Bussy' Coldicott which is saying a good deal. His nickname 'Cherub' did not perhaps express his personality just as faithfully as Nuttall's Dictionary does the precise meaning of the word; nevertheless it was quite a good one and contained, as Pershore nicknames usually do, quite a subtle humour. He was nice looking with an unalterable merry countenance and an infectious cheerful spirit. Therein lay the source of his popularity. He was as full of mischief as an egg is full of meat. He was the most juvenile member of the Working Men's Club and if at times his exuberant vitality led him to dance instead of play on the billiard tables, the elders could not look on that countenance and chide such conduct as of course it ought to be chided. And now he is dead, his roguish pranks and audacious sayings are everywhere recalled in affectionate memory and with many a sigh that he will never in his life be seen or heard again.

Two years ago when he was 17 years of age, he joined the Worcestershire Yeomanry as bugler and as he persistently expressed his desire for more active service – quite in keeping with his character – he was eventually transferred to the Worcesters. He had only been out in France seven weeks before he met his death. But he saw a good deal of fighting in that time and wrote and told his Mother how he put his first German hors de combat. Major Blew, the Commander, in a letter to the parents bears out exactly that estimate of his character which this little report has endeavoured to imply:-

'It is a sad letter I have to write you to express my deep sympathy to you in the sad loss of your boy who was my cheery little trumpeter for so long during the weary months of training. I heard from his Sergeant who wrote and told me of his death and how he fought and died acting up to the highest traditions that have made the name of the Worcester lads so famous. I knew he was the right stuff and you have every reason to be proud of him. I should like you to know the esteem of your lad was held in by his mates and officers and that you and your family are not alone in your grief. I shall never have another trumpeter like him'. A good deal of sympathy is felt for Mr & Mrs Coldicott in the loss of their youngest boy. It is only a year ago since their third son, Alfred, also of the Worcester died in Parkhurst Hospital, Isle of Wight. Another son, Harry of the Royal Field Artillery is at the front while the eldest son, Will, who was formerly a Butler to Bishop Gore is working in a munition factory".

Private Alfred COLDICOTT
Service No 1405
Age: 19
4th Battalion Royal Warwickshire Regiment
Died aged 19 in training on 6th March 1915. Buried with military honours at Cowes, Isle of Wight.
Buried in Parkhurst Military Cemetery, Grave III. F. 72.
Son of Alfred and Jane Coldicott of Broad St, Pershore

Evesham Journal 13th March 1915 – DEATH OF A PERSHORE SOLDIER

"We regret to record the death of Pte. Alfred Caldicott, the third son of Mr & Mrs A Coldicott of Broad Street, Pershore which occurred on Saturday last at Cowes, Isle of Wight. Pte. Coldicott was twenty years of age, joined the Army some years ago but left the service on account of heart trouble. On the outbreak of war however, he re-joined his old regiment the 4th Warwickshires and was stationed with them at Warwick until his regiment was moved to the Isle of Wight. The first intimation the bereaved parents received that their son was took ill was by wire on Saturday and Mrs Caldicott at once took the train to Cowes. She was, however, too late to see her son alive. The funeral took

place at Cowes on Tuesday afternoon. Pte. Caldicott's early death is greatly deplored by his many friends while deep sympathy is expressed for his parents and relatives. Pte. Caldicott's younger brother is a bugler in the 1st Reserves Worcester Yeomanry and is at present stationed at Worcester."

Lance Corporal Thomas COLDRICK
Service No 23562
Age: 28

7th Battalion Gloucestershire Regiment
Killed in action in Mesopotamia on 18th December 1915.
Born in Gloucester and was a resident of Pershore.
Enlisted in Gloucester. Left England 5th September 1915.

Thomas Coldrick

Husband of Ellen Costins (formerly Coldrick nee Clarke), 13 Park Head Rd., Dudley, Worcestershire formerly of High Street in Pershore.

Evesham Journal 6th January 1917 (Continued from the George Thomas Coldrick entry) "Lance –Corpl. Thomas Coldrick of High Street has been officially reported to have died of wounds in Mesopotamia. Much sympathy is felt for Mrs Coldrick. The Lance-Corpl who was 28 years old, joined two years ago as a Territorial but in a few months was discharged as medically unfit. A short time afterwards, however, he joined up with the Gloucesters and went through the Gallipoli campaign. He contracted trench fever here and had six months in hospital in India. It was only recently he was sent out to Mesopotamia. Previous to the war, Lance-Corpl. Coldrick was employed at the Atlas Iron Works in Pershore and before that he was ostler at the Royal Three Tuns Hotel".

Private Harold CONN
Service No 15585
Age: 19

1st Battalion Royal Fusiliers
Died of wounds at Flanders on 29th December 1916.
Buried in Bethune Town Cemetery, France
Grave VI. A. 46.
Second Son of Edward & Ellen Conn of 1, Victoria Terrace, Pershore

Evesham Journal 13th January 1917 – ANOTHER PERSHORE LAD's DEATH.

"Pte. Harold V Conn of the Royal Fusiliers has Fallen in the fight. His parents, Mr and Mrs Edward Conn of Victoria Terrace, Pershore, received the authoritative report this week that he was wounded in France. The matron of the hospital wrote expressing her sympathy and stated that the surgeon did all that he could to save his life but the case appeared hopeless from the first. He died without regaining consciousness and was buried with military honours in the cemetery, a little cross marking his last resting place. This happened on December 29th.

A fortnight before Mr and Mrs Conn heard from him and he then said he was going into a rest camp and should probably be home for his Christmas dinner. Pte. Harold Conn had seen two years of the war and yet was only 19. He was a strapping 6ft tall young fellow and though he had been through some of the hottest of the fighting, he always wrote the most cheerful letters home. Prior to the war, he was a gardener in the employ of Mrs Gauntlett, Ash Villa and afterwards for Mr W T Chapman. Mr Conn's eldest son, Pte. Edward Thomas Conn of the Worcesters is also lying wounded in a hospital in Hertfordshire".

Private George Henry COSNETT
Service No 5503
Age: 19
1st/5th Battalion Somerset Light Infantry
Formerly 30254, Dorsetshire Regiment
Died of disease on 18th November 1918 in Egypt.
Born and enlisted Pershore. 2nd/4th Dorset regiment
Egypt went out October 1917,
Buried in Alexandria (Hadra) War Memorial Cemetery,
Egypt, Grave E. 196.
Son of George & Harriett Cosnett of Head Street,
Pershore

Private Henry William COSNETT
Service No 70421
Age: 19
2nd Battalion Devonshire Regiment
Died of wounds on 28th May 1918 at Flanders.
Born and enlisted Pershore, Worcestershire. Worked at

Summerton's. Left England about 30th April 1918.
Buried in Marfaux British Cemetery, France, Grave V. D. 2.
Son of Mrs Elizabeth Cosnett of Newlands, Pershore

Private John COSNETT
Service No 36162
Age: 30
1st Battalion Welsh Regiment
Formerly 13930, 3rd Battalion South Wales Borderers
Died of wounds on 27th May 1915 in Flanders France.
Born and resident Pershore, Worcestershire, enlisted at
Newport, Monmouthshire Buried in Bailleul Communal
Cemetery Extension (NORD), France, Grave I. B. 42.
Son of Thomas & Amelia Cosnett, Church Street, Pershore

Evesham Journal, February 13 1915 _[continues on from the notice of Thomas Herbert Cosnett's death] :-- A BROTHER WOUNDED._

"Private John Henry Cosnett, another son of the family, has just come home invalided. He belongs to the South Wales Borderers, and his regiment took part with the troops of Japan in the battles which deprived the Germans of the important island of Tsing-tau. Here he was twice wounded, in the shoulder and foot., the latter wound necessitating his coming home. He brought home the portrait of his regiment taken in Japanese uniform, which the British soldiers all had to wear to prevent the enemy finding them out, for here again it was against the English that the fiercest hatred was concentrated. Private Cosnett speaks enthusiastically of the fighting powers of the Japs, and said our men got on wonderfully well with them. Mr. and Mrs. Cosnett have five more sons serving under the colours, and their eighth son, George, recently offered himself, but was certified medically unfit."

Evesham Journal 31st August 1915 - News has lately come that Pte. John Cosnett of the South Wales Borderers, is home from the Dardanelles and is lying badly wounded in Royal Hospital at Salford, Manchester. He is the third son of Mr & Mrs T H Cosnett of Church Street, Pershore who have given seven sons to the Army, surely a local record. As was reported in this paper some few months back, the second son was Pte. Thomas Herbert of 2nd Worcesters who was killed in France so now there is but six. Pte. John Cosnett, now wounded at Manchester, was with his regiment when the English, in collaboration with the Japs, brought about the fall of the German island Tsing-tau on 7th November last. That was an important and memorable exploit to have taken part in and after a few days' furlough at home he was sent out to the Dardanelles in February. His Mother went to Manchester to see him last week.

Private Thomas Herbert COSNETT
Service No 8467
Age: 31

2nd Battalion Worcestershire Regiment
Died of wounds on 19th January 1915 at Flanders
Born and enlisted Pershore, Worcestershire. First to Go from the Town. One of seven sons of Thomas & Amelia Cosnett who all Joined up. The King sent Congratulations on 30th November 1915.
Buried in Bethune Town Cemetery, France, Grave III. B. 57.
Son of Thomas & Amelia Cosnett of Church Street, Pershore

Evesham Journal, 13 Feb. 1915:-- PERSHORE SOLDIER'S DEATH.

Private Herbert Thomas Cosnett, one of the seven soldier sons of Mr. and Mrs. T.H. Cosnett, of Church-street, Pershore, died on the 29th ult. from wounds received while in action the previous day, The Colonel of the ``D'' Company 2nd Worcesters wrote acquainting the parents with the sad circumstance, and Lord Kitchener's black-edged letter has also been received by them expressing the ``true sympathy of his Majesty and the Queen in their sorrow.''

Another letter, also much treasured by Mr. and Mrs. Cosnett, came from Private William Sharpe, of the same regiment, who evidently saw the last of their son. He wrote: ``Poor Bob was a devoted friend of mine ever since we came to France. A bullet hit him while in action: he died the next day, and was buried with military honours in the town cemetery at Bethune. I must say no one could have shown a braver spirit than Bob; he set an example to all. My comrades and I very much miss him, and greatly sympathise with you in your bereavement.''

Private Bob Cosnett was the second son of his parents, and had seen *twelve years in the army. He served throughout the Boer War, and though taking part in several engagements he was lucky enough then to come through scathe less. He went to France with the Expeditionary Force, and therefore took his share in those fierce early engagements, than which there has been nothing since more creditable to the glory of British arms. He wrote many letters home, in which he was always optimistic that he should get through all right, a prediction unfulfilled. Like thousands more ``Tommies'' he was intensely proud of Princess Mary's gift of a pipe and box of tobacco with which was a charming little card wishing the soldiers a Happy Christmas and a Victorious New Year. These gifts he sent home to his father, with the injunction to keep them safe, a request which, needless to say, will now be regarded with greater significance than ever.*

Gunner William Charles Samuel CROOKE
Service No 831438
Age: 25

"B" Battery 306th Brigade, Royal Field Artillery
Died of wounds on 23rd May 1918 at Flanders .
Royal Field Artillery. Son of Sergeant Brooke, Bridge
Street, Pershore. Married Mrs Rusher's cook. Went
out 1st May 1916. Buried in Pernes British Cemetery,
France, Grave II. C. 16.

William Crooke

Pershore Abbey War Memorial - surname spelt Crook
Worcester Post Office Wainwright Road - surname spelt Crooke
Husband of Elizabeth Mary Crooke of The Paddock, Pershore.

Evesham Journal, 1 June 1918:-- PERSHORE SOLDIER DIES OF WOUNDS.

Gunner William Charles Crooke, R.F.A., the eldest son of Sergt. and Mrs. S. Crooke, of Bridge-street, Pershore, died in the Canadian Clearing Station, France, on May 23 from his severe wounds received in action a few days before. In the first letter to his wife (who lives at the Paddock, Pershore) the Chaplain (The Rev. J.R. Tibbot) said; ``Will wishes me to say he isn't hurt very much, but I must warn you that his condition is serious''. Later the Chaplain wrote in sympathetic terms announcing his death, his burial in the British Cemetery, and giving the number of the grave. He added that his severe injuries were shell *wounds in the lower part of the abdomen, that he rapidly weakened, and when the end came his mind was not clear, as he left no messages for home.*

Many letters of sympathy has been received both by Mrs. Crooke and the parents. A comrade (Gunner E.J. Chapman) wrote ``Will was the most popular chap in his battery. He was always in good spirits and his ready wit and keen sense of humour saved the situation on several occasions. I can't express to you how much we shall all miss him".

Gunner Will Crooke had been more than two years in France, and though in several big battles escaped injury till he received the grave wounds that ended his career. He came home on a short furlough in February last, and was then married to Miss Bennett, of White Ladies Aston, for whom much sympathy is felt. The parents too, who feel their loss acutely, are deeply sympathised with. Sergt. S. Crooke is now stationed in Ireland. Their youngest son died in a convalescent home a few months ago, and this month their second son Charles, just 18, was called up. Mr. Crooke's mother died last July, and Mrs. Crooke's mother shortly before.

Evesham Journal 6 July 1918 :-- HOW GUNNER W.C. CROOKE DIED.

In a letter to Mrs. W. Crooke of Pershore, Major Penny, commanding `A' Battery of the R.F.A., says:- ``It is with great sorrow I write you with reference to the sad death of your husband, Gunner W.C. Crooke. He was hit by a shell on his way to the observation post and died in hospital on the same day. He had been a member of this battery for three years, over two of which he had served under me in France, always carrying out his duties faithfully and well. Hard working, with a contempt for any danger, and always cheerful, he was very popular with officers and men, and will be greatly missed by all."

Private Albert William Thomas DANCOCKS
Service No 39226
Age: 22
1st Battalion Royal Berkshire Regiment
Killed while being carried from the field wounded at

Flanders On 30th November 1917
Commemorated on Cambrai Memorial, Louverval,
France, Panel 8.
Son of Thomas & Sarah Dancocks of High St., Pershore

Evesham Journal 29th July 1916 – "Mr and Mrs T Dancocks of High Street have received official information that their eldest son Pte. Albert W T Dancocks of the Worcesters has again been wounded. He is in hospital in France. Pte. Dancocks, who is but 21 years of age, has been in the trenches 16 months and has been thrice wounded. It is said he was the first to join Kitchener's Army in Pershore. The Father, Mr Thomas Dancocks, is an old soldier."

Evesham Journal 23rd December 1916 – PERSHORE MAN WOUNDED.

"Pte. Albert Dancocks of the Worcesters, son of Mr and Mrs T Dancocks of High Street is officially reported wounded and this makes the third time. He has now been wounded in four places by shrapnel and lies in a serious condition in Cambridge Hospital. Pte. Dancocks was the first recruit from Pershore under Lord Kitchener's first call for men".

Evesham Journal 24th March 1917 – FROM A PERSHORE BOY.

"We have received an interesting letter from Pte. A Dancocks of the Royal Berks who tells us that he is a Pershore boy. He says he is a reader of the 'Journal' and has learnt through this paper of many of his comrades being killed or wounded and he wishes to express his deepest sympathy with all his Evesham and Pershore friends, whose sons or husbands have fallen in the great war. As to his adventures, he says that he joined the Army on 31st August 19 and after doing six months training at Plymouth he went to France at the end of March 1915 and joined the Worcesters of which regiment he will always be proud. Her served for three months around Ypres and was not sorry when he went elsewhere. His next place was Ploeg-Street near Messines which he describes as a picture palace compared with Ypres. Then he went back for a rest to a village names Penin and after his rest went up to Vimy Ridge and 'Oh it was Vimy too'. You could not walk along without the ground shaking beneath you, it was so much

under-mined. The first night we had it was quiet. On the second night up went a mine and we lost a platoon.'

WOUNDED. *He goes on: 'IT was at Vimy where I received my first wound, being hit by a German sniper in the right knee and the finger of the left hand while we were holding a crater. I had done fifteen months without a scratch. I was glad to get away from the trenches for a little while, if only to have a rest. I did not get home that time but re-joined my battalion. After another rest, we went down to the Somme. After a long march we got to a wood just behind Thiepval and I can say it was warm too. After a few days there we went down to Albert, upon a field up above the town, and stayed there for a night and then up into a charge at La Boiselle. At the taking of La Boiselle I got wounded for the second time, this time in the right shoulder. I was glad to get away for a time and was sent down to the base at Rouen. I did not like being down at the base so as soon as I was able I volunteered for the front again but instead of going back to my old regiment I was sent to the Royal Berks. I was very sorry to leave the good old Worcesters but never mind, I may get back there some day.'*

HIS THIRD WOUND. *'It was then we went up to Devil Wood. Known as Devil's Wood but we did not stay there long. We went back to some village for a rest and after that we went to a place called Couin just behind the firing line. Then we did a bit of trench work for about three weeks and afterwards went back to train for a charge which we had to do. We did the training and went back up to the trenches at Beaumont Hamel. It was in this attack on 14th November that I got wounded for the third time, this time being hit in the left side and left hand. Thus it was this time I got home and I was very glad to get there for a rest and to see the people at home. I have been to Evesham and found it quite quiet to what it was before the war'.*

Evesham Journal 19th January 1918 - PERSHORE MAN KILLED

"On the 28th ult. Mr and Mrs T Dancocks of High Street, Pershore were officially informed from the Warwick Record Office that their son, Pte. Albert W T Dancocks of the Royal Berkshire Regt. was posted as missing on 30th November. They had previously received the news from a letter which Pte. George Smith sent to his Mother at Pershore but their anxious enquiries have now elicited the grave information of his death.

This news was sent by Sergt. Stacy of the Berkshires. In his letter to the parents he says "As No 7 Platoon Commander, I have had your letter asking information respecting your son handed to me, I have made the fullest enquiries possible and learn from several men that he was killed while going back to the dressing station wounded. I am very sorry to have to tell you this news but I think it is much better to hear the worst at once. I was in charge of the platoon at the time he was wounded and the Sergeant himself was killed. I've had enquiries from other people about him and will write to them also. I hate writing such bad news and offer you my deepest sympathy".

It is said that Private Dancocks was the first in Pershore to join Kitchener's Army. After seven months training, he went with the 3rd Worcesters to France where he went through some of the biggest battles and was twice wounded through the head, back and thigh. Pte Albert Dancocks, who was but 23 years old, was the son of an ex-soldier who has done 28 years with the colours but who, as he himself says, did not see so much fighting during the whole course of that time as his son experience in a couple of minutes. Before the war, Pte. Dancocks worked at Atlas Works. A younger Brother (Harold) in a bandsman in the 6th Worcesters. Pte. Dancocks once wrote to the Journal describing his experiences"

<u>Evesham Journal 15th June 1918</u> - *PERSHORE MAN'S DEATH*

A communication from the Record Office, Warwick confirms reports sent by comrades of Pte A W T Dancocks of the Royal Berkshire Regt. son of Mr & Mrs T Dancocks of High Street, Pershore, that he was killed in action last November. Pte. Dancocks was one of the first to join up and went through scores of engagements, being wounded several times. being wounded several times".

Lieutenant Robert Hartley DEAKIN

Age: 22
10th JATS and 45th Squadron Royal Flying Corps
Died on 22nd July 1917 near Cassel France.
Scholar of Cheltenham Grammar School - Captain of his house. Undergraduate at Jesus College, Oxford.
Gazetted to Indian Army from Sandhurst
Commemorated on Arras Flying Services Memorial,

France.

Son of William Robert and Mary Jane Deakin, of Norton Hall, Worcester

Further information on Robert Deakin available online at:
http://www.deakin.broadwaymanor.co.uk/deakin/robert-hartley-deakin.html

Private Walter John DOLPHIN
Service No: 50583
Age: 19

2nd Battalion Royal Berkshire Regiment

Died at Flanders on 11th August 1918

Taken prisoner 27th May 1918 having gone to France January 1917. Buried in Niederzwehren Cemetery, Germany, Grave VIII. F.10

Son of John and Alice Dolphin of 3 Church Row, Pershore

Private Herbert Henry DUFTY
Service No 39736
Age: 20

4th Battalion Worcestershire Regiment

Formerly 2870 Worcestershire Yeomanry

Born and resident Pershore, enlisted Worcester

Killed in action 26th November 1916 at Flanders.

Appears on Worcester Guildhall, Worcester St Clements Church, Worcester Post Office Wainwright Road, Pershore Abbey memorials.

Commemorated on Thiepval Memorial, France, Pier and Face 5A and 6C.

Son of Postman Frederick & Jane Dufty of Little Priest Lane, Pershore

Grandchild of Mrs Barber, Church Street

Lance Corporal William James DUFTY
Service No 16952
Age:20

1st Battalion Grenadier Guards

Awarded Distinguished Conduct Medal

Killed in action on 17th October 1915 at Flanders.

Lance Corporal, Grenadier Guards, D.C.M.
Commemorated on Loos Memorial, France, Panel 5 to 7.
**Son of Captain Hudson's man, Mr & Mrs Andrew
Dufty of Victoria Terrace, Pershore.**

Evesham Journal 12th June 1915 - DCM FOR PERSHORE MAN

We are pleased to give publicity to the honour which has come to Lance-Corporal W F Dufty, a Pershore lad, serving the Grenadier Guards. Though not yet twenty years of age, he has taken part in much fierce fighting in France and has now been recommended by his Commanding Officer for the Distinguished Service Medal. Lance-Corporal Dufty is the son of Mr Andrew Dufty, late of Pershore, and who is now coachman for Capt. M Hudson of Birlingham.

He has sent the following letter he received home to his parents:-

"May 28th. Pte.. W Dufty - Your Company Officer and Brigade Commander have informed me that you have distinguished yourself by conspicuous bravery in the field on 16th May 1915. I have read the reports and have forwarded them to higher authority for recognition. Promotion and decoration cannot be given in every case but I should like you to know that your gallant action is recognised and how greatly it is appreciated. Signed H P GOUGH. Commanding 7th Division".

With reference to this notable communication enclosed, Corpl. Dufty thus writes to his Mother:-

"I am sending you a paper I received the other day from our C.O. The General commanding our Division thanked me for what I did in action. As I told you in my last letter, this was for throwing bombs up at trench which the Germans were in. 3 of my poor comrades were struck down but I managed to get missed again. Just my luck. You will see by the paper I may get the D.C.M. so you may yet be proud of me. You will also notice that I have been made a Lance-Corporal." Lance Corporal Dufty as a member of the Pershore Boy Scouts and a leader of the Company when the Rev. Hawkes Field was Scoutmaster.

Evesham Journal 11th September 1915 - D.C.M. FOR PERSHORE MAN

Lance-Corpl. William James Dufty, the 2nd son of Mr Andrew Dufty of Pershore, has been awarded the Distinguished Conduct Medal for bomb-throwing in Flanders. His many friends in the Pershore District are delighted to learn of the honour conferred upon him and many have sent their congratulations to the parents. Lance-Corpl. Dufty was only 20 years of age last Good Friday but he joined the 1st Grenadier Guards nearly 12 months before the war broke out. Prior to that he was in the employ of Mr G R Hammond, Fruit Grower, of Pershore. He went out to France with his regiment last November and has seen much fierce fighting and though he has not been injured so far, he has recorded home some miraculous escapes. His eldest Brother, Pte. John Dufty in the Royal Artillery, is now supposed to be on his way home from India to the front."

Evesham Journal and Four Shires Advertiser, Saturday, September 18, 1915:

Lance-Corpl. W.J. Dufty, of the Grenadier Guards, the second son of Mr. and Mrs. Andrew Dufty of Pershore has been awarded the Distinguished Conduct Medal for gallantry while engaged in bomb throwing in Flanders.

DCM Citation:
16952 Private W.J. Dufty, 1st Bn., G. Gds. (LG 5 Aug. 1915)
For conspicuous gallantry on the 16th May, 1915, at Festubert, when, with the Company bombers, he was engaged in bombing up to 300 yards of trench. The bombers and one section under a Non-Commissioned Officer successfully blocked and held the trench after the bombs had run out. Private Dufty showed the greatest courage and resource, and gave a fine example of devotion to duty.

Corporal Walter EDWARDS
Service No 240491
Age: 34
1st/8th Battalion Worcestershire Regiment
Born in Pershore. He landed in France on 1st April 1915. Gassed on the Somme repairing a section of the road on 20th July 1916. Returned to the unit on 8th December 1916 Killed in action at Flanders on 5th October 1918Served in Italy August 1918.
Buried in Beaurevoir British Cemetery, France,

Cpl W. Edwards, Pershore. Killed.

Grave C. 29. Name appears on: Pershore Abbey,
Kempsey St Mary's Church
Husband of Rose Edwards of Worcester Road, Pershore

Second Lieutenant Sidney Fitzroy D FELL
Service No 2662
Age: 24
12th Battalion attached 3rd Battalion Worcs Regiment.
Killed in action on 10th July 1916 at Flanders.
Commemorated on Thiepval Memorial, France, Pier
And Face 5A and 6C.
Appears on: Worcester Guildhall - appears twice,
Worcester Cathedral Choir Memorial Window,
Pershore Abbey
Husband of Mrs Jessie Fell of High Street

Evesham Journal 22nd July 1916 –

_"News has been received officially that Lieut. S F Fell was killed in the
recent fighting. He was a son of the late Mr R Fell of Fellcourt County
Cork._ _He had lived at a suburb of Hereford before he came to
Worcestershire seven or eight years ago._ _He lived for a time at
Pershore where he was a member of the Abbey Choir and of the
C.E.M.S. Later he came to Worcester and he was articled to Mr
Arrowsmith Maund but the outbreak of war cut short his legal studies.
He was a member of the Cathedral Voluntary Choir and was
associated with the St John Scouts._ _When war broke out, his
patriotism first found expression in organising the Public School Boys'
Corp with whom he left the city._ _He was afterwards given a
commission in a Worcestershire Battalion._ _He was employed for a long
time in a training camp in Devonshire and crossed to the front only a
month ago._ _In January 1915 he married Miss Dowty, daughter of the
late Mr WW Dowty Chemist, Pershore and Sister to Mr W W Dowty
photographer, Pershore."_

Private Harry FLETCHER
Service No 9295
Age: 22
"B" Company 1st/8th Battalion Worcs Regiment
Killed in action aged 22 on 13th March 1916
Buried in Le Touret Memorial, Pas de Calais, France.

Appears on: Pershore Abbey, Little Comberton War Memorial, Little Comberton St Peter's Church
Son of William and Annie Fletcher, Lt Comberton.

Private Alfred Ernest FULCHER
Service No 8956
Age: 28
2nd Battalion King's Shropshire Light Infantry
Died on 17th February 1917 in Salonika, Greece
Born St Peter's, Worcester, enlisted Worcester
Buried in Pieta Military Cemetery, Malta, Grave D. XVII. 6.Ganderton's Entry. Shropshire Light Infantry.
Appears on: Worcester St John in Bedwardine Church, Worcester Guildhall, Pershore Abbey
Husband of Jane Brant of Newlands, Pershore

Lee-Cor. A. E. FULCHER, Shropshire L.I. (Died.)

Evesham Journal, 4 June 1917 - ``DIED ON HIS WAY BACK." Mrs. Fulcher, of the Newlands, Pershore, has received notice that her husband, Lance-Corpl. A.E. Fulcher, of the Shropshire Light Infantry, died on board the vessel which was taking him back to join his regiment at Salonika. Lance-Corpl. Fulcher, who was 28 years of age, had been twice wounded in action in France, He had served 9 years with the same regiment. Only two months ago he married the daughter of Mr. G. Brant, of Pershore, and much sympathy is felt for her."

Private Henry GARRETT
Service No 7278
Age: 36
3rd Battalion Worcestershire Regiment
Killed in action aged 36 on 1st June 1916 at Flanders.
Born at Pershore. Went out to the Front in 1914.
Buried in Ecoivres Military Cemetery, Mont-St. Eloi, France, Grave III. A. 8.
Son of Mrs Emma Pugh of Church Street, Pershore

Sergeant Frederick GEORGE
Service No 11737
Age: 21
1st Battalion Worcestershire Regiment
Killed in action at Flanders, France on 18th February 1915 Lance Sergeant, 1st Worcesters

Born & resided in Pershore, enlisted Worcester
Buried in Guards Cemetery, Windy Corner, Cuinchy,
France, Grave VIII. E. 6.
**Son of Edmund & Sarah George of High St,
Pershore**

*Evesham Journal, 27 February 1915:-- A PERSHORE SERGEANT
KILLED.*

*Pte. J.E. Stanton of the 1st Worcesters writes us from France as
follows under date February 20th:- ``I am writing you these few lines to
thank you for the two copies of the `Evesham Journal' which you have
been kind enough to send out to me each week, and which I have
received quite safely. I may say I hand them on to T. James, E. Smart
and R. Knight, who are Evesham chaps in the company, also to E.
Hughes of Pershore. I am sorry to say that the sergeant over our
platoon was killed on the 18th last. He was Sergt. F. George, and came
from Pershore, and he was very much liked by both the men and
officers, and he is one who will be greatly missed. We have been
having a lot of wet weather out here lately, which of course makes the
trenches in a very bad state, but yesterday and today have been tow
grand days, and we are now beginning to look forward to better
weather. Again thanking you for the good old `Journals' which I may
say we always look forward to"*

Evesham Journal 6 March 1915:-- PERSHORE SOLDIER'S DEATH.

*Pte. J.E. Stanton's letter from France sent to the ``Journal" and
published last week, was the first information Pershore people had of
the fate of Sergt. Fred George of the 1st Worcesters. Since then the
official intimation of his death has been forwarded and the deepest
regret is generally felt at the loss of another gallant Pershore lad.*

*The deceased was the younger of the two sons of Mr. Edmund
George, of Pershore and a handsomer boy or finer looking soldier has
never donned khaki. Though but 21 years of age, he had served
several years in the service and was stationed in Egypt when war was
declared.*

In his school days, which seem but yesterday, and for a short time afterwards when he was residing at home he took the keenest interest in Pershore hockey, and was no mean exponent of the game. His pleasant manners, good looks, and sportsmanlike attributes made him a great favourite with all, and none will give a sadder or kindlier thought to his memory than his old colleagues, the members of Pershore Hockey Club.

HOCKEY PLAYERS IN KHAKI. It will not be irrelevant to enumerate here the name soft other Pershore hockeyites in whom the love of contest and conquest has shown itself on so many a pleasant mead in various parts of the county, who when the sterner call of their country's need came answered readily and willingly:-- Messrs. C.H.Lushington, C.E.Slater, W.H.Taylor, H.Mumford, A.Gray, J.Staynor, R.Wagstaff, J.Lord, H.Sharpe, F.Wood, J.Knight, L.Hook, D.Hook, C.W.Hellier, Hiram Moulson and possibly one or two more, whose names cannot be recalled at this moment. And a large percentage of the remainder of the members of the Club chafing under the disagreeable truth of that unfortunate phrase ``Too old at 40" applicable alike to military as well as industrial interests, have sought what peace of mind they can get by joining the local Voluntary Training Corps.

Lance-Corporal Arthur GILES
Service No: 240731
Age: 33
Lance Corporal, 1st/8th Worcesters.
Died of influenza at home on 27th November 1918.
Appears on: Pershore Abbey, Pinvin St Nicholas
Church, Pinvin C of E School under Naunton
Beauchamp Buried at St Nicholas Church in Pinvin,
Pershore.
Son of Edwin & Sophia Giles of Head St, Pershore
Husband of Mary Giles of 2 Deerhurst Terrace, Pinvin

Gunner Albert Mark GILES
Service No 106924
Age: 25
42nd Battery 2nd Brigade Royal Field Artillery
Killed in action on 21st March 1918 by a stray bomb
amongst The horses at Flanders, France. Born in
Pershore, enlisted in Newark, Nottinghamshire

Mark Giles

Commemorated on Arras Memorial, France, Bay 1.
Son of Edwin & Sophia Giles of Head St, Pershore

Evesham Journal 18th May 1918 - PERSHORE MAN KILLED

Mr Edwin Giles of Head Street has received official intimation that his son, Gnr Mark Giles RFA has been killed in France. In a very sympathetic letter to the parents, Major Nicholls said that a stray shell fell among the heroes and Mark was killed instantaneously. The Major added that Mark had served his battery faithfully and well and he could not adequately express the deep regret he felt at his loss. Gnr Giles was 25 years of age and prior to the war worked for the National Railway Company. Mr Giles has 3 other sons with the colours, Alfred in the Grenadier Guards, Fred in the Gloucesters (Italy) and Lance-Corpl. Arthur Giles now in Italy."

Private Joseph GRINNELL
Service No 15662
Age: 37
10th Battalion Gloucestershire Regiment
Formerly 15583, Oxfordshire & Buckinghamshire
Light Infantry. Killed in action on 13th October 1915
at Flanders, France. Born in Pershore, married Sarah
Webb in 1898 in West Bromich. Enlisted at Birmingham
Went out 8th August 1915, killed 13th October 1915.
Commemorated on Loos Memorial, France, Panel 60 to 64.
Husband of Sarah Webb of West Bromich.
Son of Charles & Maria Grinnell of Oldbury.

Private George William GRINNELL
Service No 240280
Age: 26
1st/8th Battalion Worcestershire Regiment
Killed in action on 26th August 1917 at Flanders.
Enlisted at Pershore. Commemorated Tyne Cot
Memorial, Belgium, Panel 75 to 77.
Son of Charles and Jane Grinnell of Head St., Pershore
Husband of Mary Ann Grinnell

William Grinnell

Evesham Journal 15 September 1917 - ``PERSHORE CASUALTIES.

Three more well-known Pershore lads have lately made the great sacrifice. All were Williams, and belonged to the fighting Worcesters. Pte. William Grinnell fell on the 26th August. Lieut. J.R. Willis, in a letter of sympathy to his wife, who lives in Pershore, says he was killed instantaneously by a shell while outside his dugout. The lieutenant adds, `He was a company signaller, and consequently is a great loss to us. It is only the best men who are picked to be trained as signallers' Pte. Grinnell was mobilised at the very beginning of the war, and had seen and experienced the horrors of much bitter fighting. Three more brothers, who are the sons of Mr. Charles Grinnell, Head-street, are with the colours, namely, Sergt. C.L. Grinnell, who has been at the front and is now in England; Pte. George, now home from France; and Pte. Albert, who now lies wounded in hospital. Pte. Grinnell leaves a wife and one child."

Private John GRINNELL
Service No 8033
Age: 28
3rd Battalion Worcestershire Regiment
Killed in action on 16th June 1915 at Flanders.
Born and resident of Pershore, enlisted at Besford
Commemorated on Ypres (Menin Gate) Memorial,
Belgium, Panel 34.
Son of Charles and Cecilia Grinnell of Newlands,
Pershore. Husband of Rose of Reddings Row,
Church St, Pershore.

Evesham Journal 26 June 1915:-- PERSHORE MAN DIES OF WOUNDS.

"On Thursday Mrs. Grinnell, of Pensham, Pershore, received the news of the death of her husband, Private Jack Grinnell, of the 5th Batt. 3rd. Worcesters. The sad intelligence came on a postcard as follows:--

``Dear Mrs. Grinnell, - it is with deep regret and pain I write to tell you that your husband, Jack Grinnell, has died from the effects of wounds received in battle. Cheer up, and do not let this worry you too much. He died an honourable death, fighting for his children and yourself. I am his chum, Pte. Ernest Kingham, and thank God I have so far managed to come through it all right.

Though no official information has been received, Mrs. Grinnell is obliged to accept it as being only too true. She had been accustomed to send her husband a parcel every week, and he when writing home frequently mentioned how much this same chum enjoyed a share of the things she sent. Pte. Grinnell was twenty-eight years of age, and leaves two small children, one three years old and the other twelve months. He was a special reservist, and was called up and sent to France on the outbreak of war. Wounded in the hand, and with frost-bitten feet, he was declared unfit for service, and came home in December last. He was called up and sent out again before the year was out. Formerly Pte. Grinnell managed the garden plantations of Mr. Blythe at Pensham."

Private John Francis GRUNDY
Service No 325441
Age: 22
Queen's Own Worcestershire Hussars (Worcester Yeomanry)
Killed in action in Egypt on 23rd April 1916
1st/1st Worcester Yeomanry, embarked at Avonmouth
9th April 1915 for service with the Mediterranean
Expeditionary Force, disembarked at Alexandria.

John Grundy

Commemorated on Jerusalem Memorial, Israel,
Panel 3 and 5. Appears on: Worcester Cathedral, Worcs Hussars & Pershore Abbey
Worked at Messrs Phillips & Sons of High St, Pershore.
Mentioned in R C Edwards' letter in the Evesham Journal on 29th December 1917 that he'd been killed around Easter Sunday 1916 in the same action that had resulted in R C Edwards' capture by the Turks.
Son of John & Florence Grundy of High St, Pershore

Gunner Arthur HALL
Service No 831784
Age: 32
61st Division Ammunition Column Royal Field Artillery
Killed in action on 6th September 1917 at Flanders.
Born and enlisted Pershore, Worcestershire
Buried in Vlamertinghe New Military Cemetery,
Belgium, Grave IX. H. 27.
Appears on: Pershore Abbey & Worcester Post Office

Son of Arthur & Susan Hall of Priest Lane, Pershore

Evesham Journal, 22 September 1917 (contd. from Harry Baylis entry)

"While one mother gets news that brings comfort, another gets tidings that cause poignant sorrow. Mrs. Hall, of Priest-lane, who, too, is widow, has had official intimation that her son, Arthur, a gunner in the Royal Garrison Artillery, has been killed in France.

Less than two months ago Arthur was home on leave, and was married to Miss Colley, who used to be manageress of the International Stores, Pershore, and who holds the same position for the firm in her native home of Leominster. The aged mother and the young widow have the deepest sympathy of all who know them. Gunner Hall, who was a fine strapping young fellow, was attached to Pershore Post Office before joining the colours.

He was a valued member of Pershore Abbey choir, and in his service last Sunday, the Vicar made reference to him. He was also a member of Pershore Amateur Dramatic Society."

Corporal Ernest HALL
Service No 12418
4th Battalion Worcestershire Regiment
Killed in action aged 24 on 6th August 1915 in Gallipoli
Born Pershore, Worcestershire 2nd Worcesters.
Commemorated on Helles Memorial, Turkey, Panel 104 to 113.
Son of Thomas & Sarah Hall of Newlands, Pershore

Captain George Meysey HAMMOND
Age: 25
Australian Infantry, A.I.F.
28th Bn. Died on 14th June 1918 of wounds at Morlancourt,
France
Son of Mr George Richard Hammond & Emily Hammond nee Roberts of High St, Pershore

Evesham Journal 2nd September 1916 "A WOUNDED ANZAC – Mr & Mrs G R Hammond of High Street, Pershore have received intimation that their only son,

Sergt. Maysey Hammond of the Australian Infantry Forces has again been wounded and is in a base hospital in France. Sergt. Hammond was previously wounded at the Gallipoli Peninsula. Many residents in Pershore, besides his parents, will be gratified if he is fortunate enough to recover from his injuries and come home safe from conflict. Sergt. Hammond is a young man of much promise, who, with sheer hard study and determination, fitted himself for good positions in the Civil Service. He lived for six years in North-West Australia and when the war broke out was employed in an administrative department in Broome. He joined the Australian Infantry a little more than two years ago and went through the horrors of Gallipoli, where, as before mentioned, he was wounded.

His last letter from France states 'I received a dose of shrapnel in my left leg on the glorious night when the battalion went over the top. The Doctors have extracted the stuff but goodness knows when I will commence crawling about again. I do so want to get back to the good old 28th instead of lying so helpless here. We had a hell of a time. There is only 30 of us left, so perhaps a fellow must count himself extremely lucky to come out with only a leg wound. All our officers have gone and I'm rather anxious to know what they propose doing with the small remainder of the company.

Evesham Journal 23rd September 1916 "AN ANZAC'S PROMOTION – Mr George Maysey Hammond, only son of Mr and Mrs G R Hammond of High Street, Pershore, has been promoted from the rank of Sergeant to that of Second Lieutenant 'for services in the Field'. Lieut. Hammond, who belongs to the Australian Infantry Forces, is at present lying wounded in hospital in France, having received his injuries during the recent offensive. He was previously wounded at the Gallipoli Peninsula. Lieut. Hammond went to Australia in 1911, and passing fifth out of a huge number of candidates for the Commonwealth Public Service (Post Office Branch) was appointed to a post at Broome, NW. He joined the Army in March 1915 and has been on active service ever since. His many friends at Pershore will be glad to hear of his promotion".

Private George Hamilton HANDS
Devonshire Regiment Service No: 37690
Age: 36
Formerly Lancashire Fusiliers Service No: 47034
Formerly Royal Army Service Corps Service No:
R/449862. Born 1882 in Oxfordshire
Died in Killingbeck Military Hospital on 1st February
1918 Of Trench Fever.

Chaplain Frank Robert HARBORD
Age: 49
Royal Artillery Chaplain 4th Class.
Army Chaplain's Department. Attached 25th Division
Chaplain's Depot.
Died from wounds on 8th August 1917 near Ypres.
Vicar of Dunchurch, Rugby.
Also served as Chaplain during the Anglo-Boer War.
He was made Deacon in 1890 and Priest in 1893 by the
Bishop of Bloemfontein. He then held various appointments in the
Orange River Colony. Acting Chaplain to the Forces in the Boer War,
1900-02. Curate of Yorktown and Camberley 1909-10, Pershore 1910-
12, Vicar of Dunchurch from 1912. He is commemorated in his former
parish church at Dunchurch. A plaque commemorates his service in
the South African war and a magnificent stained glass window was
paid for by his wife in memory of his WW1 service. Chaplain 110
Brigade R.F.A. Died one year after joining up.
Buried in Brandhoek New Military Cemetery, Belgium, Grave V. A. 1.
Son of William E. And Mary Harbord; husband of Edith C. Harbord
Husband of Edith Clara Harbord of Southern House, Broad St,
Pershore

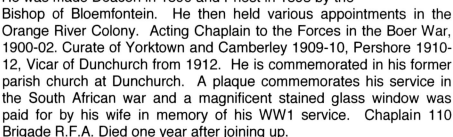

Saturday 25th August 1917: CASUALTIES TO LOCAL OFFICERS -
REV. F.R. HARBORD

Rev. Frank Robert Harbord who died of wounds on August 8, while
serving with the R.F.A., was vicar of Dunchurch, near Rugby, and prior
to that was curate of Pershore. He was 49 years of age, and was the
youngest son of the late W. Engledow Harbord, of the Manor House,
Sutton. He was preparing for Cambridge when he had a breakdown in
health and was ordered to South Africa where he took Holy Orders.
For many years he was stationed in the Orange Free State, and for two

years was an acting chaplain with the forces in the Boer War. On the outbreak of the present war he volunteered for service but was not called up until August 1916, and had completed exactly a year of service abroad on the day of his death. He had just arranged for a further extension of leave from his parish, and in one of his last letters home wrote:- "I cannot leave the Army when the hardest fighting is to take place."

Lance-Corporal William George HAYNES
Service No 4034
Age:32
Worcestershire Regiment – 1st/8th Battalion.
Died of wounds at Flanders, France on 15th December 1916. Commemorated on Becourt Military Cemetery, Becordel-Becourt I.F. 2
Husband of Mrs Ellen Haynes of Newlands, Pershore
Son of Henry & Mary Haynes of Newlands, Pershore
Evesham Journal 6th January 1917 – "MORE PERSHORE MEN KILLED.

George Haynes

"Two more names have been added to Pershore's Roll of Honour. Mrs Haynes of the Newlands, has been officially informed that her husband, Lance-Corpl. George Haynes of the Worcesters has been killed in France. A letter from Capt. Gist speak of him as a 'splendid type of soldier, an excellent leader of men and one who will be greatly missed by all the officers, non-commissioned officers and men of his company'. Lance-Corporal Haynes was certainly a popular young fellow in Pershore and many will grieve that they will never see him in this life again. He was one of the best exponents of soccer football the town has produced, which is saying a good deal considering the name Pershore has had for the sporting spirit for a number of years. He invariably played centre or left to a good many clubs in the district as well as Pershore for he seemed to find delight in playing occasionally against his old colleagues. Lance-Corpl. Haynes benefitted considerably under the wills of two Pershore Uncles and at the time of his death held reversionary interest in a great deal of property, land and tenements. He leaves and widow and four children."

Lance Corporal Ernest Walter HAYNES
Service No 17103
Age: 26
11th Battalion Worcestershire Regiment
Killed in action on 24th April 1917 in Salonica, Turkey.
Prior to joining the 11th Battalion Worcs Regiment
he worked for Mr Mumford. He was reported missing
on 24th April 1917. Commemorated on Doiran Memorial,
Greece. Worcester Cathedral Cloister Windows Bell Ringer.
Son of George and Sarah Haynes of Three Springs Rd, Pershore

*Evesham Journal 16th June 1917 - Corpl. Ernest William Haynes of the
Worcesters, son of Mrs S Haynes of Three Springs Road, Pershore, is
reported missing. He was probably in the same fight as the late Sergt.
Need" (note the discrepancy in names)*

GDSN William Henry HITCHINGS
Service No 21323
Age: 21
Grenadier Guards 3rd Battalion.
Died at Flanders, France on 8th February 1917
Enlisted at Pershore. Lived in Wickwar, Glos. In
1911, his Occupation is listed on the Census as
"Apprentice Grocer"Buried Grove Town Cemetery,
Meaulte, Somme.
Son of Arthur and Malinda Hitchings of The Buthay, Wickwar

Lance-Corporal William Douglas HOOK
Service No 1941
Age: 22
Royal Warwickshire Regiment 1/6th Battalion-Territorial.
Died of wounds at Flanders, France on 13th February
1917. Commemorated at Bray Military Cemetery,
France
**Son of Sergt. Major Richard & Mrs Fanny Hook of
High Street, Pershore.**

Douglas Hook

Evesham Journal 24th February 1917 -CORPL. HOOK KILLED

*"Scarcely a week passes but what additional names have to be added
to Pershore's Roll of Honour, which now numbers 54. The latest is*

Corpl. Douglas Hook, who it is officially announced to the parents, has succumbed to wounds received in action on the 4th inst. He died on the 13th at No. 5 Casualty Clearing Station, France, at the age of 22 years.

Corpl. Douglas Hook was the youngest son of Sergt. Major Richard Hook of Pershore, was one of the smartest of the many that Pershore has sent out. He belonged to the Signal Section of the Royal Warwickshire Territorial Regiment, mobilised in August 1914. After experiencing 20 months' hard fighting in France, he was wounded on July 1st 1916 in one of the battles on the Somme. He was in the General Hospital at Oxford for four months having received serious shrapnel wounds in the side and arm. He returned to France at the end of the year. His death will be genuinely lamented throughout the district for he was widely known and very popular. He possessed in a full measure the sporting spirit characteristic of the family. He played football, hockey, cricket, while as a runner he had many successes. He won the Boy Scouts' race for three successive years at Pershore Flower Show. He was an old Choir boy of Pershore Abbey. Hubert, the eldest son of Sergt. Major Hook, is still serving in the trenches and Louis, who went through the Gallipoli campaign as a Sergeant in the Worcestershire Yeomanry, is now at home."

Major Arthur Cyril HUDSON
Age: 36
Royal Fusiliers (City of London Regiment)
Died of wounds on 2nd October 1916 at Flanders,
France. Commemorated at Boulogne Eastern
Cemetery, VII A.2.Pershore Abbey, Wick War
Memorial, Wick Church
Son of Colonel Alfred & Lydia Hudson of Wick
Manor.
Husband of Irene Hudson

Arthur C. Hudson

Evesham Journal 31st August 1915 - MAJOR A C HUDSON
WOUNDED

News has been received at Wick House that Col. Hudson's second son, Major Arthur C Hudson of the Royal Welsh Fusiliers was wounded when fighting in Northern France last week. The Major had only been in France a week or two and this was his first experience of warfare. The shot struck him in the arm just as he was leaving the trenches after successful bombing of the enemy's lines. He was removed to the base hospital and now has just arrived at a London hospital.

<u>*"The Times" Thursday, October 5, 1916*</u>,

"Major Arthur Cyril Hudson, Royal Fusiliers, who died on October 2, of wounds received in action during the previous week, was the third son of Lieutenant-Colonel A.H. Hudson and Mrs. Hudson, of Wick House, Pershore. Educated at Clifton College, he joined the South Staffordshire Regiment in 1900, and served in the South African War. At the conclusion of the war he was gazetted to the Royal Fusiliers, and served in India with the 2nd and 3rd Battalions of that regiment. At the outbreak of the present war he was on leave in England, and was attached for duty to a Service Battalion of the same regiment, in which he was promoted to the rank of major. He came home wounded in 1915, and returned to the front in February last. He married in 1908, Irene, daughter of the Rev. H. Clifford, of Endon Hall, Pershore, and leaves one son."

<u>*Evesham Journal 7th October 1916*</u> *"DEATH OF MAJOR ARTHUR HUDSON"*

"An official telegram to Wick House on Saturday morning announced that Major Arthur Hudson had been seriously wounded and was in hospital at Boulogne. A second telegram in the evening of the same day at Endon Hall reported the words "Seriously wounded" and authorised Mrs Hudson, the Major's wife, to go to France. Too late for the last train that night, Mrs Hudson commenced her journal by the earliest on Sunday morning but the Major had passed away before she reached France. He died that day and the sad announcement was officially made to Colonel Hudson early on Monday morning.

Major Hudson of the Royal Fusiliers was the second son of Col. And Mrs Hudson and son-in-law of the Rev. H & Mrs Clifford of Endon Hall, Wick. He married Miss Irene Clifford, their eldest daughter, at Evesham about eight years ago and the hearts of all classes of people in Pershore go out in sympathy to both families, who are now suffering this deep personal sorrow, for the young widow and her child, and especially for Col. And Mrs Hudson who now mourn the loss of two out of three of their soldier sons.

Their younger son, Lieut. Aubrey Hudson of the Worcester Regiment, was killed in the battle of the Aisne, September 20th 1914. Major Warren Hudson, also of the Worcester, is at Salonika. The late Major Arthur Hudson served through the South African War, getting the Queen's medal and clasp. He joined the Royal Fusiliers in 1902 as a second lieutenant. When war broke out in 1914 he was home on leave with his regiment from India. He was wounded at Loos in 1915 when taking part in a successful bombing raid on the enemy's lines. He had been in the Somme fighting since July and it was here he received his death wounds. He was thirty-six years of age. His Father, Colonel Hudson is Regimental Commandant of the Worcestershire Volunteer Movement and his Father-in-Law, the Rev H Clifford, is commandant of Pershore and District Platoons."

Lieutenant Aubrey Wells HUDSON
Age: 31
5th Battalion attached 2nd Battalion
Worcestershire Regiment
Died on 20th September 1914 at Aisne, France.
Commemorated on La-Ferte-Sous-Jouarre
Memorial, France. Pershore Abbey, Wick War
Memorial, Wick Church
Son of Colonel Alfred & Lydia Hudson of Wick Manor.

Aubrey W. Hudson

Berrow's Worcester Journal, 3rd October 1914:

Lieut. A.W. Hudson is the youngest son of Lieut.-Col. A.H. Hudson, of Wick House, Pershore. He is 31 years of age. He served for several years with the Cape Mounted Rifles, in South Africa, under Col. Lukin, and was transferred in 1909 to the 5th Worcesters (Special Reserve). On the outbreak of the War he was appointed to the 2nd Battalion of the Worcesters for active service and he has been present at all the engagements, including Mons. Two other sons of Col. Hudson are in the Army, viz., one in the Royal Engineers and the other in one of the Worcestershire Service Battalions of Kitchener's New Army.
Berrow's Worcester Journal, 10th October 1914: Wor'shire Casualties - Death of Lieut. Hudson.

The family of Lieut. Aubrey Hudson (who last week reported missing) have received an official communication from the War Office that he is dead.

Deep sympathy is extended by a large circle of friends in the district to the family in their bereavement. At the harvest festival service on Sunday in Pershore Abbey, the Rev. J. Jervis, Vicar of Wick, made a touching reference to his death, and to the toll of human life in the European War.

Lieut. Hudson was the youngest son of Col. A H Hudson of Wick, Pershore. He was 31 years of age. He served for several years with the Cape Mounted Rifles in South Africa under Colonel Lukin. He was transferred in 1909 to the 5th Worcesters (Special Reserve). It will be remembered that the Special Reserve, numbering about 600 officers and men, were encamped at Croome Park this summer, and that, on the day war was declared by Great Britain against Germany, Lord Coventry presented to the Battalion its new colours, and Lieut. Hudson was told by his Commanding Officer to receive the colours from his Lordship. Lieut. Hudson was appointed to the 2nd Battalion of the Worcester's for active service, and had been present at all engagements, including Mons. He was serving with the Second Division of the 5th Brigade, which has just been commended by Field Marshall Sir John French for its excellent work. Lieutenant

Hudson was very popular in the Pershore district, where his family is held in universal esteem. A keen sportsman, he occasionally followed the Croome Hounds, and often played for the Pershore Hockey Club. He also associated himself various social movements in the district.

Two other sons of Col. Hudson's have Answered the call of the King and Country in this War. Capt. Arthur Hudson is serving with the 7th Royal Fusiliers, and Lieut. W. W. Hudson is serving with one of the Worcestershire Service Battalions of Kitchener's New Army.

Berrow's Worcester Journal, 17th October 1914: LATE LIEUT. AUBREY HUDSON

Sir, - I am enclosing the copy of a letter which I have received from Colonel Westmacott, who is officer in command of my son's Regiment. I have received so many kind inquiries from my son's friends since he has been reported "missing," asking for further information regarding him, and as reports have been so misleading, I am sending you a copy of his Colonel's letter, which contains the particulars of his death, and I should be very grateful if you would kindly insert it in your paper this week.

Yours faithfully
A.H. Hudson

(Copy of letter from Colonel Westmacott,
Commanding 2nd Worcesters, to Lt.-Col. Hudson).

"My dear Hudson, - I am very sorry to have to tell you, but I think you know it already, that your son, Aubrey, was killed, and please accept my sincerest sympathy.

He was getting on so well and fell at the head of his men in a wood fight, in which his Company got somewhat scattered. Many men were missing for some time. I heard afterwards from a N.C.O., who saw him fall, that his end was merciful and painless.

His body was afterwards found by some men of another Regiment and buried in the wood. We know the spot, and it can be approximately identified after the war. I am, of course, not allowed at present to give the whereabouts. I am so very sorry.

We have not as yet received very much for the men in the shape of comforts by reason of the very inconvenient postal arrangements, but these are getting better every day, and we may expect them now at any time. We do not require any clothing as Government give the men as much as they can carry. Cigarettes, papers, tobacco, chocolate, matches, etc. are what are most needed.

We are all very fit and well and getting on famously. Many thanks for all your good wishes.
Yours very sincerely,
C.B.L. WESTMACOTT"

Berrow's Journal October 14th 1916:

The late Major A C and Lieut A W Hudson

A memorial service was held in the Parish of St Bartholomew on Wednesday afternoon for Major Arthur Cyril Hudson and Lieut. Aubrey Wells Hudson, sons of Col. And Mrs Hudson of Wick House. The service was of a most impressive character. It will be remembered that Lieut Aubrey Hudson fell in the early stages of the war when the Worcestershire Regiments, to whom he belonged, suffered heavy losses. For some time there was an uncertainty as to his fate and for that reason it was deemed expedient by the family that no memorial service should be held. Recently there came news that Major Arthur Hudson had died and a memorial service for both was decided upon. Before the arrival of the family, a large number of friends of the deceased assembled in the Church while the Organist Mr G Sherwood played "The Lord is mindful" and "O rest in the Lord".

The clergy present were: Archdeacon Peile (Great Comberton) Rev W D Lowndes (Little Comberton) Rev F R Lawson (Fladbury) Rev A H Phillips (Pershore) Rev H B S Fowler (Elmley Castle) Rev H Wilkinson (Cropthorne) Rev R J Torrens (Vicar of Wick). Amongst others present in the church were Col Miller, Capt. Derbyshire, Lieut Shelmerdine, Captain Mogridge Hudson, Mr & Mrs Hammond (Little Comberton), Mrs Whiteley, Mrs Hughes, Mr A C Goddard, Mrs J Dowson, Dr M Woodward, Miss Woodward, Mrs Hugh Robinson, Mrs Smyth, Mrs H B Emerson, Miss Duke, Mr and Misses Dowson, Mrs Rusher, Dr J Rusher, Mr G Whitaker, Mrs Fuller, Dr O Wynne Marriott, Mrs Adams, Mr C Willinck, Major Thackwell, Miss Thackwell, Mrs R S Bagnell and a large number of villagers. Col Edwards and Major Sandbarn were also present.

The members of the family present were: Col A H and Mrs Hudson, Mrs Arthur Hudson, Mrs N Shelmerdine and Miss Gwyneth Hudson, Mrs Warren Hudson, Mrs Bagnall O'Caban, Miss Hemming, Rev and Mrs Clifford, Misses Clifford and Lieut. U Shelmerdine.
The service was full choral, the Wick choir having been augmented with the boys from Pershore Abbey. The service opened with the hymn "For all the Saints" followed by the General Confession after which the Lord's Prayer was repeated.

The 121st Psalm "I will lift up mine eyes unto the hills" was chanted. The Rev F R Lawson then read the special lessen from St John xxi The "Nunc Dimittis" was chanted to the setting by Fulford after which the Creed was repeated.

Archdeacon Peile then gave an address in which he paid high tribute to the brave men who had laid down their lives in this world war. He said the suffering and desolation of the war was appalling and if there were no Christ, there would be no light and no answer. We counted those as truly happy who had laid down their lives for the cause. For them, there was no more watching, waiting or pain and we now found ourselves beginning to thank God we had delivered these our brothers from sorrow and sighing. It is for us not to sorrow as men without hope. Following the address, a special prayer was said for the two gallant officers. Then the hymn 'Peace, perfect peace' was sung and prayer was then offered by Archdeacon Peile in which the gallant Worcestershire Regiment was mentioned. The hymn 'Lord while afar our brothers fight' was sung. After which the Benediction was pronounced by the Archdeacon Peile. Before the family and congregation left the church, the 'Last Post' was sounded from outside the church by Drummer Vant from Norton Barracks. As the congregation left the church the organist played Hadel's 'Largo'.

Private Edward James Hughes
Service No 9035
Age: 25
Worcestershire Regiment 1st Battalion
Born in Flint. Enlisted at Pershore, was living in
Worcester. Killed in action on 13th March 1915 at
Flanders, France Listed on Le Touret Memorial. Pas
de Calais, France.

Private Philip HUNT
Service No 27767
Age: 34
Royal Warwickshire Regiment 1/7th Battalion
Died of wounds at Flanders France on 8th October 1917
Listed on Tyne Cot Memorial.
Son of George & Hannah Hunt of Bridge St,
Pershore

Private Albert Trimwell JONES
Service No 57927
Age: 18
Worcestershire Regiment 2/8th Battalion
Killed in action at Flanders, France on 1st November 1918
Valenciennes (St Roch) Communal Cemetery
Grave 111.D.15
Son of Hensor & Grace Jones of Priest Lane,
Pershore

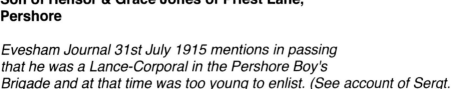

Evesham Journal 31st July 1915 mentions in passing
that he was a Lance-Corporal in the Pershore Boy's
Brigade and at that time was too young to enlist. (See account of Sergt.
Biddulph)

Lance Corporal Arthur R KINGS
Service No 18015
Age: 22
Grenadier Guards 1st Battalion
Died of wounds on 21st November 1916 at Flanders,
France Carnoy Military Cemetery Grave X.19
Son of Mr & Mrs Joseph Kings of Gas Walk, Pershore

Arthur R. Kings

<u>*Evesham Journal 19th Feb 1916*</u> *"CHAMPION BOXER"*

"Since the war started, four Pershore lads were in that fine Regiment,
the Grenadier Guards, namely Lance-Corporal W J Dufty who won the
DCM for bomb throwing in Flanders and who, soon after distinction as
conferred upon him was killed while giving a further exhibition of British
pluck and tenacity; Pte. Percy Smith who never got over the terrible
wound in the head he received during a fierce engagement and died in
a London Hospital; Pte. W Kings who though he was in the first
Expeditionary Force to France and has taken part in several of the
hottest fights, has so far escaped without a scratch and his Brother Pte.
Arthur Kings who was put out of action at the battle of Loos with a
bullet through his arm.

While in France, Pte. Arthur Kings won the boxing championship of his
regiment and received 50 francs. He has been to Pershore lately on a
brief furlough and was far more communicative and excitable about his

boxing that his adventures in fighting the Huns. Visiting his old haunt, the Working Men's Club, Pte. Arthur persistently endeavoured to get members to engage him in a little honourable contention with the gloves. But each and all promptly refused, which is not to be wondered at seeing the challenger stands at 6ft 3in high, turns the scale at 13 stone, is as fit as the proverbial fiddle and possesses a fist fashioned after the similitude of a leg of mutton. He has now returned to the fighting line in France."

Evesham Journal 9th December 1916 PERSHORE MAN KILLED

"Mr and Mrs Joseph Kings of the Gas Walk, High Street, Pershore has received official intimation that their son, Lance-Corpl. Arthur Kings of the Grenadier Guards, has been killed in action. The news first came to the parents through the Chaplain of the regiment, Rev. Leslie Palmer, who is a very sympathetic letter stated the Lance Corpl. Was brought to the dressing station unconscious and that he remained in that condition until he died shortly afterwards. Arthur Kings was as popular in the army as he was out of it and at Pershore, had a host of friends; he will be greatly missed.

In stature, he was a veritable giant standing 6ft 3in in his socks and proportionately built. He was good at sporting games, had an excellent record for running with the Birchfield Harriers and was a winner of many local competitions. He won a name for the art of boxing and just after he was sent to France he carried off the prize of 25 francs as champion of the heavy-weight competition promoted by the officers. He joined the army in September 1914 and exactly a year later was wounded at Loos.

For about a year he received hospital and convalescent treatment. He was 22 years of age. He was formerly in serve at Messrs. Phillips and Sons of High Street, who entertained a high regard for him for his steadiness, reliability and courtesy. Messrs Phillips, it may be stated, have had seven of their original staff join the colours, three of whom have died for their country, the other two being troopers Jack Grundy and Arthur Bozzard of the Worcestershire Yeomanry."

Private Arthur John LANGFORD
Service No 27869
Age: 24
Worcestershire Regiment 3rd Battalion
Killed in action on 9th October 1916 at Flanders.
Listed on the Thiepval Memorial, Somme, France.
Also listed on the Paxford War Memorial in Glos.
Son of John & Sarah Langford of High Street, Pershore

Arthur Langford

Evesham Journal 4th November 1916 - PTE. A LANGFORD KILLED.

"Pte. Arthur Langford of the Worcesters, who was killed on October 9th by the bursting of a shell in the trenches, was a Pershore man and the youngest son of the late Mr John Langford, who for a quarter of a century was foreman at Atlas Iron Works.

Pte. Langford, who leaves a widow and one child, lived at Paxford where, before he joined the Army, he was manager for Messrs. Jas. Slatter & Co Cider Merchants.

The deceased young soldier, who was only 24 years of age, joined up in April last and three months later was sent out. He was in the notable fight on 24th August when the gallant Worcesters routed the much-vaunted Prussian Guard. Here it was that he saw a Pershore comrade, Pte. Leonard Preece, lying dangerously wounded with a shattered thigh and rendered him timely aid.

Mrs Langford at Paxford has received a most kind and sympathetic letter from Lieut. Davis, who said he personally felt the loss of Pte. Langford very keenly , as he was a good soldier and a pattern to his comrades. The Chaplain (the Rev G M Evans) also wrote, saying he buried him in the little cemetery behind the lines and that a handsome wooden cross marks his last resting place. The grave, he adds, will always be carefully looked after.

The late Pte. Langford's Mother, for whom much sympathy is generally felt, resides in the High Street Pershore."

Lieutenant Cecil Henry Gosset LUSHINGTON

Age: 31

"A" Company 10th Battalion Worcestershire Regiment
Born on 16th December 1884 in India
Killed in action on 3rd July 1916 at Flanders
Son of Major Arthur James Lushington &
Constance Caroline Lushington, of The Park
Sandling, Maidstone, Kent.

Evesham Journal 22nd July 1916

Evesham Journal 22nd July 1916

"News has been received that Lieut. Cecil H Lushington is wounded in hospital. He was a prominent fruit grower in this district, being a pupil of Mr E P Whiteley."

Evesham Journal 5th August 1916 – LIEUT. C H LUSHINGTON

Lieut CHG Lushington of the Worcestershire Regiment, who was officially reported to be 'wounded and missing on 3rd July 1916' has now been officially reported to have been killed in action. He was 31 years of age and was educated at Winton House, Winchester and at Haileybury College. He had been growing fruit at Pershore for some years and on the outbreak of war, he at once applied for a commission in the Worcestershire Regiment and was gazetted to a 2nd lieutenancy in September 1914. He proceeded with his regiment in July 1915 to France where the battalion saw much service in the trenches, suffering very heavy losses in officers and men. During this attack, though wounded in both legs, Lieut Lushington declined assistance and he appears to have been lost sight of at the time. From an unofficial source, however, it is reported that he was subsequently seen to be hit again and received a fatal wound to which he succumbed in a few minutes. In referring to his death, one of the officers under whom he served wrote 'He was a splendid officer and his men always loved him and would have followed him anywhere. He had the very highest form of courage; he realised danger but never shirked it.' He was a good cricketer, a free and forcing bat and made several high scores for the Gentlemen of Worcestershire. He was also a good hockey and lawn tennis player. He was the younger son of Major and Mrs A J Lushington of Bampton House, Oxfordshire and married, in February 1915, Evelyn M Hirst, the only daughter of Mr & Mrs F J Hirst of Oathurst, Bampton, Oxon."

Private Nicholas J MANN
Service No 9543
Age: 37
Worcestershire Regiment – 9th Battalion
Killed in action on 15th December 1916 at
Mesopotamia, Commemorated on the Basrah
Memorial, Iraq. Listed Tewkesbury War Memorial,
Pershore Abbey
Son of Clr. Serjt. Nicholas and Sarah Mann of Tewkesbury
Husband of Annie Mann of Newlands, Pershore

Nicholas J. Mann

Evesham Journal 30th December 1916 – PERSHORE CASUALTIES

"Mrs Mann of the Newlands, Pershore received the sad news from the War Office on Boxing Day, the anniversary of her wedding day, that her husband Pte. Nicholas Joseph Mann had been killed in Mesopotamia. Pte. Mann belonged to the Worcesters and was 38 years of age. His wife had not seen him since just before he sailed for the Dardanelles, a year and six months ago.

He was badly wounded in Gallipoli and was four months in hospital. Mrs Mann is left with three children. Pte. Mann's younger Brother, Sergt. Victor Mann, was killed in France last August and another Brother, Lance-Corpl. Frank Mann, after being four times wounded is again back in the trenches. The Father, Nicholas George Augustus Mann is an Irishman and a good patriot. He lives at Tewkesbury and although 75 years of age, belongs to the V.T.C. It should be stated that Pte. Mann was a Volunteer in the South African War, for which he has medals and clasps, and he also volunteered in the early days of the present war. Prior to this he was an agent of the Pearl Insurance company at Pershore."

Evesham Journal 6th January 1917 – TEWKESBURIANS KILLED

"Pte. Nicholas J Mann of the Warwicks. Was killed in action on 13th December. Deceased was the eldest son of Col. Sergt and Mrs Mann of Tewkesbury and leaves a widow and three small children who reside at Pershore to mourn his loss.   He was one of the first batch of Tewkesbury Volunteers to serve in the South African War and was well known in Tewkesbury where he was for some years in the employ of

Gunner Charles MARSHALL
Service No 183338
Age: 21
Royal Field Artillery – "D" Bty. 306th Bde.
Died at Flanders, France on 7th May 1918
Buried at Gonnehem British Cemetery, Pas de Calais,
France
Son of Charles & Ellen Marshall of Newlands,
Pershore of

Evesham Journal, 1 June 1918:-- PERSHORE CASUALTIES.

Each week sees additions made to the Pershore Roll of Honour, now a formidable list. Signaller C. Marshall R.F.A. eldest son of Pte. and Mrs. C. Marshall, of the Newlands, was killed in France on May 7. He was 21 years of age and unmarried. Before enlistment he resided with Mr. and Mrs. W. Guest, bakers of Rounds Green, Oldbury, by whom he was employed, and who held him, as their letters show, in great esteem. Every member of the Rounds Green staff have written in sympathy to the parents. Before working there, he was with Messrs. P.J. Prothero & Co., Pershore.

The circumstances of his death were related in a letter from Lieut. E. Millward, who writes:- ``He had not been long in my section, but had proved to be an efficient and cheerful worker, and one of our best telephonists. It may be some consolation to you to know he suffered no pain, being killed by a shell which dropped on our cook's fire.

His best friend, Gunner Barker was killed, at the same time, and both are buried side by side in a cemetery close by. Our own padre took the service, all of us being present. The Father, Mr Charles Marshall, was this week discharged from the army after 3.5 years' service. Another son, Will, is serving in the front line

Private Edward J Marshall
Service No 43693
Age: 23
Lincolnshire Regiment – 10th Battalion
Formerly 4660 Worcestershire Rgt.

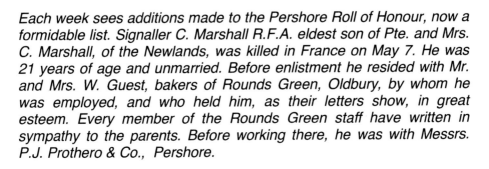

Killed in action of 28th April 1917 aged 23 at Flanders.
Listed on Arras Memorial, France
Son of John & Rose Marshall of Newlands, Pershore
See Samuel James Annis for report on death.

Lieutenant Kenneth Ralph Mason
Age: 27
4th Bn. Suffolk Regiment
Killed in action on 21st June 1915
Buried at St. Vaast Post Military Cemetery,
Richebourg-L'avoue, Pas de Calais, France
Son of George and Loetitia Mason of Ipswich

*Evesham Journal 29th July 1916 mentions that Lieut.
Kenneth Mason (killed in France) had been a
member of the Pershore Hockey Club.*

*Evesham Journal June 26 1915:-- PERSHORE LIEUTENANT KILLED.
News was received in Pershore yesterday (Friday) morning that Lieut.
Kenneth Mason had been killed in action. Lieut. Mason was formerly a
pupil of Mr. E.P. Whiteley, and a year ago purchased from the exors. of
Mrs. Grewcock the gardens at Gigbridge, Pershore*

Corporal Arthur MAYO
Service No 203377
Age: 31
2nd/7th Battalion Worcestershire Regiment
Killed in action on 3rd December 1917 at
Flanders.
Buried in Fifteen Ravine British Cemetery,
Villers-Plouich, France, IV. G. 10.
Born and enlisted Pershore.
Was a Postman previously.
Went abroad 6th October 1916.
Appears on: Pershore Abbey, Worcester Post
Office Wainwright Rd
Son of Mrs Ellen Mayo of High Street, Pershore

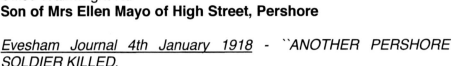

Arthur Mayo

*Evesham Journal 4th January 1918 - ``ANOTHER PERSHORE
SOLDIER KILLED.*

One of the latest Pershore men who is reported to have made the great sacrifice is Corpl. Arthur Mayo (Jackie Mayo he was always called by his chums, and he had many who valued his friendship).

Capt. Williams, who commands his company, in a letter of sympathy to Mrs. Mayo, who lives at the Old Turnpike House in Bridge-street, said the corporal was a most reliable soldier and an expert with the Lewis gun. He was with a few men on outpost duty when a shell exploded on the edge of his position, causing wounds from which he died shortly afterwards. The captain added that he would be much missed by the company. Corpl. Mayo was attached to the staff at Pershore Post Office, and three of his colleagues have been killed before him, while one is a prisoner of war. Corpl.

Mayo was home on furlough a short time since, and met his death within a week of his return. He was good at most kinds of sports, and excelled in football.

Lieut. Col. John Francis James B Miller
Age: 72

Royal Engineers Indian Staff Corps.
Born in Bombay.
Died on 7th January 1917 of Pneumonia
Worked as a recruiting Officer during WW1
Buried in Pershore Cemetery.
Lived at Amerie Court in Newlands, Pershore
and is on 1901 Census for Little Comberton.
Husband of Mrs Grace Miller nee Guest

Berrow's Worcester Journal: Death of Col. Miller – S. Worcestershire Recruiting Officer

Lieut-Colonel James Frederick Miller died at his residence in Amerie Court, Pershore on Sunday morning. He was aged 72. Exactly a week ago, he contracted a chill and pneumonia supervened. On December 20th 1916, he married at the Abbey Church Miss Grace Guest, daughter of Mr Thomas Guest of Pershore, who is attached to the Royal Engineers.

The death of Col. Miller is everywhere regarded with regret. He was the Recruiting Officer for the South Worcestershire Sub-Area and he performed his duties with efficiency, discretion and kindliness.

By his first wife, he leaves a daughter. Mrs J B Dowson of The Poplars, Bricklehampton, a lady who is extremely popular with all classes of society in the country and whose many acts of kindness are gratefully remembered in the households of the poor.

It is about 20 year since Colonel Miller and his daughter went to live in the Pershore District. For half that time they resided at The Cottage, Little Comberton. He was a keen follower of the Croome Hounds.

Col. Miller was a Staff Officer of the Indian Army and as an Engineer he did good work in the construction of roads and in connection with schemes of irrigation.

The funeral took place at the Cemetery on Wednesday afternoon and was of a semi-military character. The preliminary portion of the service was held at the Abbey Church which was crowded. Some hundreds of people were also gathered round the entrance gates and afterwards followed the cortege as it proceeded to the cemetery. Signs of mourning were to be seen in all parts of the town, shutters being put up at most business places and blinds being drawn at private houses.

The procession started from Amerie Court at 2.30. A firing party, in command of Lieut. E C Sadler, marched in front with arms reversed. Then came the hearse containing the coffin, around which was wrapped the Union Jack and on the top were placed the dead Colonel's sword, belt and military cap. The Bearers were six non-commissioned officers (all Sergeants) from Norton Barracks.

The mourners were Mrs J B Dowson (daughter), Mrs Miller (widow), Mr J B Downson (son-in-law), Rev H Bourne (bother-in-law) Mr J W Dowson (Lower Hill) the Misses Dowson, Mr and Mrs T Guest, Master Harcourt Guest, Col C E Greenway (Head-Quarters Staff, Recruiting Area), Major Baker, Major Smith, Lieut. Neil Shelmerdine, Mr John Kent (Upton-Upon-Severn), Nurse Iremonger and Sergt. Major R Hook.

The coffin was met at the Lych Gate by the robed clergy and surplice choir and on either side of the Church Walk were drawn up the members of the Pershore, Elmley Castle and Cropthorne platoons of the Volunteer Training Crops under Commandant Rev H Clifford. Pending the arrival of the cortege and during the seating of the large congregation, Mr C Mason (the Abbey Organist) played Spohr's "Blest are the departed" and Beethoven's "Funeral March". The commencement of a deeply impressive service was the hymn "Let saints on earth in concert sing". The 90th Psalm was sung to Felton. The burial service was read by the Ven. H F Peile, Archdeacon of Warwick. The last hymn "Now the Labourer's task is o'er". Then followed the Nune Dimittis and the service ended with Chopin's "Funeral March" on the organ.

Among the congregation were The Rev A H Phelps (Vicar of Pershore) and the Rev F R Lawson (Rector of Fladbury) officiating the Rev W H Wilkinson, the Rev Harcourt Fowler, the Rev W F Oakley, Dr Martin Woodward, Miss Woodward, Lieut. Col A Hudson, Mrs Hudson, Miss Hudson, Mrs Derrington Bell, Miss Hemming, Mrs Owen Wynn Marriott, Mr H Basil Harrison, Mr W Pearce, Mrs Winstanley, Mrs Clifford, Miss Clifford, Mr J S Bagnall, Capt. Derbyshire, Mr F Cope (Evesham District Military Tribunal), Mr A E Baker (Clerk to Pershore Tribunal), Mr and Mrs A W Smith, Misses Smith, Mr Charles Hunt, Mr A C Goddard, Mrs Goddard, Mr E T Grizzell, Mr D Workman, Mrs Caldwell, Mr J Billson, Will Friend (Head Huntsman of the Croome Hunt representing Mr R S Bagnall, Hon Secretary of the Hunt).
The committal portion of the service was taken by the Vicar and the Rev F R Lawson. Here many others took up position behind the mourners, including the clerical staff from Pershore Recruiting Office.

Immediately the service concluded, the firing party fired three volleys over the grave and the "Last Post" was sounded by two buglers from Norton Barracks. The grave was lined with white chrysanthemums, ferns and moss.

Beautiful floral tributes were sent by "Enid", Mrs J B Dowson, "Jack and Children", Mrs A L Gallie, Miss Gallie (Tavistock), "George and Carrie Miller" (Stirling), Capt and Mrs Smyth (Manor House, Fladbury), "Staff from Pershore Recruiting Office", "In lasting memory, Frances Miller", Mrs F Cox, Lieut. General Sir Francis Davies, Colonel C E Greenway and officers Headquarters Staff 29th Recruiting Area, "In remembrance of comradeship", Captain and Mrs Cartland (Abbey Terrace, Tewkesbury), Lieut-Colonel A H Hudson and Mrs Hudson, Mr John W

Dowson, Misses Dowson, Mr and Mrs H Basil Harrison, Mr and Mrs T Guest, Mrs F Cox, "Indoor and outdoor servants at The Poplars" and one without a card.

Private Harold G Moseley
Service No 28688
Age: 19
Hampshire Regiment – 2nd Battalion
Died of wounds at Flanders on 5th September 1918
Buried at Longueness (St Omer) Souvenir Cemetery,
Pas de Calais, France
Son of Thomas & Lucy Moseley of Chipping Campden
Formerly of High Street in Pershore (1911 Census)

Harold G. Moseley

Evesham Journal, 21 September 1918:-- PERSHORE SOLDIER DIES OF WOUNDS.

"Deep sympathy is felt with Mr. and Mrs. T. Mosley and family, High Street, Pershore, in the loss of another son, Pte. Harold Moseley, of the Hampshire Regt., who is reported officially of having died of wounds received in action in France. He was 19 years of age. Previous to joining the colours in June 1917, he assisted his father in the boat trade. He went to France in the early part of April this year. His brother Leonard also died of wounds four months ago."

Private Leonard T Moseley
Service No 13181
Age: 22
Hampshire Regiment – 2nd Battalion
Died of wounds at Flanders, France on 6th May 1918
Buried at Ebblinghem Military Cemetery, Nord, France
Son of Thomas & Lucy Moseley of Chipping CampdenFormerly of High Street in Pershore (1911 Census)

Leonard Moseley

Evesham Journal, 25 May 1918:-- PERSHORE SOLDIER KILLED.

Much sympathy is felt for Mr. Thomas Moseley, of High-street, Pershore, an esteemed tradesman of Pershore, and Mrs. Moseley, in the death of their second son, Pte. Leonard Moseley, killed in action. At the outbreak of war, Leonard was one of the first to offer himself for the

Army, but was initially rejected. Determined, however, to enlist if possible, he underwent an operation, and in September, 1914, was accepted. He was transferred from the Worcesters, and went with a Hampshire Regt. to France in September 1915, and in December the same year proceeded to Salonika. He was invalided home in October 1916, with dysentery and malaria and was in hospital several months before going to France again in August 1917. He had just recovered from trench-fever when he met at the base his younger brother Harold, who had just arrived from England. Being devoted to his brother, Leonard asked to give up his post as a headquarter signaller, to be with him, and the request was granted. They went up the line and managed to keep together. They had only been up the line four hours when Leonard was hit by a shell and died shortly afterwards on May 6. He was 22 years of age. Percy, Mr. Moseley's eldest son, was discharged from training in 1916. The late Leonard Moseley was formerly employed at the Atlas Works Pershore, and the Midland station, at Bath

Private Arthur MOULSON
Service No 86441
Age: 28
Sussex Yeomanry 50th Battalion Machine Corps
Died at Flanders, France on 1st November 1918
Buried Niederzwehren Cemetery, Germany
(POW buried here)
Son of Frank & Mary Moulson of Glenhurst, Bridge
St. Pershore

Arthur Moulson

Evesham Journal, 21 September 1918:-- ANOTHER PERSHORE PRISONER.

After several weeks of suspense, Mr. F.W. Moulson, sanitary inspector to the Rural District Council, has received a card from his youngest son Arthur, who is in a machine gun corps attached to a Northern Regiment, stating he was a prisoner in Germany. It is about ten months ago since Mr. and Mrs. Moulson received the news that their second son, Hiram, a fine lad, exceedingly popular in local sporting circles had been killed in Palestine. Their eldest son, James, is also in the army abroad.

Evesham Journal, 28 December 1918:-- DEATH OF A PERSHORE PRISONER.

The death of Pte. Arthur Moulson, at a hospital at Darmstadt, Germany, where he was a prisoner of war, makes the second son of Mr. and Mrs. F.W. Moulson, of Pershore, have lost in the war. Hiram, a corporal in the Sussex Yeomanry, was killed in action in Palestine just a year ago. James, the eldest son, in the Wireless Section of the Royal Engineers, is now in Belgium. The late Pte. Arthur Moulson, who was 28 years of age, was in the 50th Batt. of the Machine Gun Corps. He was taken prisoner on May 27 at Crayonne, on the Chemin des Dames. His first postcard from Germany reported ``sound and well'', but in a letter one from hospital he said his leg was getting better. Very little information came from him, and a fellow prisoner at the same camp, who has safely arrived at his home in the North of England, has written in reply to Mr. Moulson that Arthur at first was put to work behind the lines, and such men were never allowed to write letters home. The parents feel their bereavement acutely. They have in their sorrow the deep sympathy of the townspeople. A few years back Pte. Arthur Moulson worked for the firm of Messrs. Prothero and co. grocers, Pershore, which place he left to take to a business left him at Bradford by an aunt, and it was from here he joined the colours.

Corporal Hiram Wilfrid MOULSON
Service No 32027
Age: 30
16th (Sussex Yeomanry) Battalion
Royal Sussex Regiment
Killed in action in Egypt on 6th November 1917
Buried in Beersheba War Cemetery, Israel,
Grave M. 34.]
Commemorated Worcester Royal Grammar School
Pershore Abbey War Memorial

Hiram Moulson

Son of Frank W & Mary Moulson, 130 Paley Rd, Bradford
Formerly of Glenhurst, Bridge Street, Pershore
Hiram attended Worcester Royal Grammar School from 1900 to 1901.

Evesham Journal 19 January 1918 - THE LATE CORPL. MOULSON.

Mr. and Mrs. F.W. Moulson of Glenhurst, Bridge-street, Pershore, has received a letter from Lieut. A. Fletcher, relative to the death of their son, corporal Hiram Moulson who was killed, as already reported, during recent successful fighting in Palestine. The lieutenant writes ``Please accept my deepest sympathy for the loss you have sustained in the death of your son. We are just back from the fighting, having a little rest, and I am taking the first opportunity of writing. Capt. Kekewich, his company commander, was unfortunately killed in the same battle, but we have earned a name which can never die, so perhaps this may be a little comfort to you in your sorrow. Your son's death is a tremendous loss to us all. Both on and off parade he was always so cheerful, a quality which accounts for so much when campaigning. I have now to re-organise the company, and my task is a great one with so many of the best lads gone, but we must hope that it will all end soon, and that the lives of these brave men will not have been sacrificed in vain"

Evesham Journal 29 July 1916 says Hiram Moulson had been a member of Pershore Hockey Club. His photograph was printed in the Journal on the 8 December 1917 (though the caption gave his name as Corpl. D. Moulson) Evesham Journal 29th July 1916 says that Hiram Moulson had been a member of Pershore Hockey Club.

Private William MUMFORD
Service No 45123
Age: 35
4th Battalion Worcestershire Regiment
Born and resident Pershore, Worcestershire, enlisted in
Worcester. Killed in action on 30th November 1917 at
Flanders. Commemorated on Cambrai Memorial,
Louverval, France, Panel 6.
Son of Mrs Eliza Mumford, Head Street, Pershore

Private John NEED
Service No 17105
Age: 23
11th Battalion Worcestershire Regiment
Born Pershore, Worcestershire
Killed in action at Salonika in the Balkans 25th April 1917
Commemorated on Doiran Memorial, Greece.
Appears on: Worcester Cathedral Cloister Windows

John Need

Bell Ringer, Pershore Abbey
Son of Verger William and Hannah Need, of Engine Terrace, Priest Lane, Pershore

Evesham Journal 16 June 1917 –

``The Roll of Honour which is attached to the door of the old Abbey Church gets larger and larger, and now assumes considerable proportions. Mr. W. Need, the verger at the Abbey, knows the names on that Roll of Honour almost by heart, and now he has the sorrow of reading thereon the name of his own son, Sergt. Jack Need, of the Worcesters, who has fallen a victim to the bullets of the Bulgarians. Writing his mother only in April last Sergt. Need, who had then been wounded, said he had been up on the high mountains of Salonika for sixteen months, and was only carried down to go into hospital. He re-joined his company in their incessant vigil again in May, and the War Office now reports him as killed. Great sympathy is felt for the parents, who have two other sons in the service, their eldest Harry, Royal Engineers, and Tom, who has been two years in France, and has been wounded, only slightly fortunately, no less than five times. These three lads were valued choristers at the Abbey Church, where their father has been a faithful servant many years.''*

Private Arthur Douglas NUTTING
Service No PLY/2325
Age: 20
2nd Royal Marine Battalion Royal Naval Division,
Royal Marine Light Infantry
Killed in action on 6th April 1918
Enlisted on 6th July 1917.
An Engineer Shaper
Embarked Royal Marine Brigade on 24th August 1917
Draft for British Expeditionary Force on 6th November 1917,
joined 2nd Royal Marine Battalion on 21st November 1917
Commemorated on Pozieres Memorial, France, Panel 1.
Appears on: Drakes Broughton St Barnabas Church, Pershore War Memorial
Son of Charles & Elizabeth Nutting of Pershore Fields, Pershore

Evesham Journal May 4 1918 - *ANOTHER PERSHORE MAN'S DEATH.*

Much sympathy is felt for Mr. Charles Nutting of Pershore Fields, who has received official information that his second son, Douglas, of the Royal Marine Light Infantry, was killed in action recently. He was, before the war, employed at the Atlas Works, and was very popular. Mr. Nutting's elder and only other son was one of the first Expeditionary Force, and he was taken a prisoner during the retreat from Mons, but is believed to have been one of the latest batch released in exchange and interned in Holland.

Private Edward George PALFREY
Service No 12827
Age: 29
Grenadier Guards – 1St Battalion
Died of wounds at Flanders, France on 5th April 1918
Commemorated at Gezaincourt Communal Cemetery
Extension
Son of Charles & Emily Palfrey of Binholme, Pershore

Berrows Journal, 14 November 1914:-- PERSHORE SOLDIER WOUNDED. THE BUTCHERY AMONG GERMANS.

Private E. Palfrey, a native of Pershore, is home invalided. He is a reservist in the 1st Battalion Grenadier Guards. He was serving in the Metropolitan Police Force at the outbreak of war, and he was called to join his regiment. He went out with the first batch of the Expeditionary Force, and consequently saw a great deal of the fierce early fighting.

In giving a description of the engagements in which he took part prior to being wounded, he says: ``Mons was the place where I got my baptism of fire. For the first two or three hours I did not know where to look or what to think about the whole affair. After that I got hardened and accustomed to the circumstances. We fought our way up a hill, on the top of which were Germans. It was awful to see the dead and wounded roll down this hill after being shot. Bullets seemed to come about us like rain. In spite of this, our commander (under Col. Carry) came out top. Later we retired to Landrecies. From there we went back to within about four miles of Paris, which was the turning point of the war. None of us ever thought we should stop the Germans getting into Paris, but by real grit and determination we sent the beggars flying back. From there we advanced, and eventually got to the rivers. We entrenched there and held the position for five days. The trenches were filled with water up to our knees, but we had to stick it. We then made a couple of bayonet charges, but in spite of this we had to retire. Although we again peppered them, we lost about 200.

After this we advanced to Soissons on the 14th September, which day I got knocked over. The Major sent two others and me to try to find the position of the outposts of the Germans. In going off, we ran up against an officer of the Connaught Rangers, who said he had sent three patrols to locate the enemy, but neither had returned. This, of course, did not look very encouraging. We advanced to about 100 yards of the sky-line when we ran up against a patrol of Uhlans, who opened fire. We then advanced and opened fire on them. They retired and we got to the top of the hill and there saw about 500 Germans advancing. We went back to the main body, and a reinforcement was sent for, as there was only about 180 of us to face them. We retired to a position to wait for them, and wait for reinforcements to arrive. We held on this position about two hours, and were eventually reinforced by two battalions.

After about five hours hard fighting they put into operation the white flag business -- which our men do not now regard. When our men advanced to make them prisoners, they opened fire on us with their big guns, causing the remnants of what was left of us to retire. They kept up a rapid fire. It was here I got wounded and several of us lay between the two fires for nearly 56 hours, not daring to move for fear of being hit again. I kept fainting, and then rousing up only to faint again. Once, on waking up, I found a couple of dead Germans laying across me. I managed to extricate myself from them. While I lay there some of the Germans watched their opportunity to crawl out and took what bit of food I had upon me. Eventually we were picked up and placed in a farm shed, where we remained two days. The wounded Germans also were brought in with us. It was here that they told me how they abominated the idea of war, but were forced into it.

After two days the ambulance came along and we were taken away from the shed. The Germans were not removed until last, and after we were got some distance away, we saw smoke and flames issuing from the farm that we had just left. Then we learned that the Germans had shelled the farm, setting fire to it and thus burned alive their own wounded. The day before we reached Landrecies we saw an *aeroplane flying over. We were ordered to lie low, so that he could not come down to try and find our positions. He came down to about 25 yards, when we were ordered to open rapid fire on him. We absolutely riddled the machine, and the airman and his mate came down with dozens of bullets in them" After being wounded, Private Palfrey was eventually conveyed about 350 miles in cattle trucks down country, and put into the General Hospital for a week, after which he was sent to England. His three wounds were from a shrapnel shell, one piece of which entered his thigh, another entered his back, and another lodged under the shoulder. The last piece is still unremoved, but he is to undergo another operation in the near future"*

Lance Corporal Francis George PREECE
D.C.M.
Service No 28667
Age:32
Gloucestershire Regiment. 13th Service Battalion
Forest of Dean Pioneer
Died of wounds on 22nd March 1918 at Flanders.
Enlisted at Chipping Campden (Was manager of
Chipping Campden gasworks) Commemorated
at
Pozieres Memorial, Somme, France. There is a
memorial to him on William Rolls' grave at
Naunton Beauchamp
NB Pershore Abbey war memorial erroneously lists middle initial as "J"
Married Ada Rolls of Naunton Beauchamp on 6th February 1907

Evesham Journal 2 February 1918 - *CHRISTMAS AT THE FRONT.*

Corpl. F.G. Preece of the H.Q. Bombers, Glos. Regt. writing form ``Somewhere in Belgium" on January 24 says:- ``I have had great pleasure of reading your paper out here in the front line trenches, and I can assure you it is a treat to get the `Evesham Journal' and see how things are going on at home. We had a very good time out here at Christmas. We happened to be out of the trenches, so we all settled down for a good time. We partook of all the usual Christmas pudding, beer, turkey, meat etc. On Boxing Day there was a Brigade Cross Country Race. The ground was covered with snow, and of course not being very far from the line the ground was very rough, but I managed to get through the lot. Nearly 200 started, I got home with ease, being *presented with a medal and winning a silver bugle from my battalion. I used to do a good deal of running in peace time round Worcestershire and Essex. My father is manager of the Pershore Gas Works, and before joining the army I was manager at Chipping Campden Gas Works, so I thought some of my friends would like to hear of my win out here at Christmas. It is a great deal different to running in England. I am pleased to say all my mates in my battalion are all going strong. We have a jolly good colonel; he is very good to us, and we are willing to do anything for him, and all the other officers are very good. We have some very rough times, but we get through them all right. We don't mean to let the Germans have their own way. I for one should be glad to see it all over, especially after leaving a wife and five children, but I would sooner fight on than give in to the Germans. Everything is done to make us as comfortable as possible. We get well fed so we cannot grumble a lot."*

<u>Evesham Journal 20 April 1918:-</u> CAMPDEN GAS MANAGER KILLED.

Official news has been received of the death of Lance-Corpl. F.G. Preece, D.C.M., of the Gloucestershire Regiment, on March 22. deceased joined the army June 1, 1916, and went out to France in December of the same year. He served as a bomber, and on February 22 of this year was awarded the D.C.M. for bravery on the field. Before joining the army, Lance-Corpl. Preece, who is the son of Mr. Preece, Manager of the Pershore Gas Works, was manager of the Campden Gas Works. He was 32 years of age, was of a genial disposition, and greatly liked by everyone with whom he came in contact. He leaves a wife and five young children.

The following is a copy of the letter received from his commanding officer - "Dear Mrs. Preece. - I am sorry to have to inform you that your husband, No. 28667, Lance-Corpl. F.G. Preece, has died in hospital of wounds received in action. He was wounded by a shell, and succumbed a few days later, though we were able to send him off to hospital within half an hour of his being hit. He was a first-class soldier, and was liked and respected by all ranks. I am pleased to be able to forward you the official announcement of the award of the D.C.M. for his gallantry while serving with the - Gloucestershire Regt. Please accept our deep sympathy with you in your great loss." A memorial service was held at Naunton Beauchamp Church on Sunday by the

Rector (the Rev. T. Davis) We shall give a photograph of the deceased soldier next week. (NB. this wasn't in the second edition, at least)

<u>Evesham Journal 4 May 1918</u>:- *HOW THE LATE LANCE-CORPL. F.G. PREECE WON THE D.C.M.*

In our issue of April 20 we reported that Lance-Corpl. F.G. Preece, of the Gloucester Regt., late gas manager at Campden, and son of Mr. Preece, manager of the Pershore Gas works, died in hospital on March 22 from wounds. Prior to his death, Lance-Corpl. Preece was awarded the Distinguished Conduct Medal for gallantry, and the deed for which he was decorated is thus officially described in the "London Gazette" of Thursday:- When in charge of a party of bombers during a raid, carrying some Bangalore torpedoes to cut the enemy wire, he joined the attacking party, and inserted a spare torpedo in a shelter full of the enemy and blew them up. His conduct was magnificent throughout."

Private Ernest PRICE
Service No 9649
Age: 41
Worcestershire Regiment 9th Battalion
Died of wounds in Mesopotamia on
21st January 1917
Buried at Amara War Cemetery
Husband of Lizzie Price, Father of 9 of Head Street,
Pershore

Ernest Price

<u>Evesham Journal 10th February 1917</u> – *ANOTHER PERSHORE MAN KILLED*

Mrs. Price, of Head-street, has received the official intimation that her husband, Pte. Ernest Price, of the Worcesters, has succumbed to wounds received in action in Mesopotamia. The widow, who is left with nine children, six of whom are dependent upon her, is deeply sympathised with in her distress. Pte. Price,, who was 41 years old, was one of those patriots who rushed to the colours in the early stages of the war. He went through the Gallipoli campaign, had been to Egypt and India, and had only recently gone out to Mesopotamia, His company officer was Lieut. Bert Hutton, of Pershore.

It was the opinion of everyone who knew him that Pte. Price was a good type of soldier, strong, determined, and not too sensitive, and was probably as good and whole-hearted a fighter as he was an industrial worker at home. For 20 years he was with Messrs. Nicholas Bros., of Pershore, who speak of him as a good and reliable servant."

<u>*Evesham Journal, 28 April 1917*</u>*, extract of an article titled `Pershore Officers':*

``A letter from Mesopotamia from Pte. Will Cowley of the Worcesters, to his former employer, Mr. Frank Nicholas, tells how Pte. Ernest Price met his death. `He was shot by a sniper in broad daylight.' `Poor old Ern,' says the writer, `I do miss him terribly. we were always chums. We enlisted together, came out here together, and only said to each other we hoped we should come home together.' The letter goes on to refer to the `smashing up' the Turks are getting."

Private William Henry PRING
Service No 20558
Age: 31
Worcestershire Regiment 9th Battalion
Killed in action on 25th February 1917 at Mesopotamia
Listed on Basra Memorial, Iraq
Husband of Ellen Pring nee Cottrill of Head Street, Pershore

<u>*Evesham Journal 28th April 1917*</u>* – PERSHORE OFFICERS*

"Pte. Wm. Pring of Pershore has been officially announced as having been killed in France. His wife, who was a Miss Cotterell of Birlingham, is left with one child".
(Note the discrepancy between his actual place of death and the notice received. Also the name Cottrill is mis-spelt.)

Private Hubert Clendon PUGH
Service No 203840
Age: 30
Worcestershire Regiment 1.7th Battalion
Killed in action in Italy on 15th June 1918
Buried Magna Boschi British Cemetery in Italy.
Memorial on Brother Thomas' gravestone in Pershore

Cemetery.
Son of Alfred & Jane Pugh of Head Street, Pershore

Evesham Journal 31 August 1918:-- PERSHORE SOLDIER KILLED.

Much sympathy is felt for Mr. Alfred Pugh, of Head-Street, who has received information that the second of his soldier sons has fallen in the war. Tom died in a London Hospital last year, and was brought home for burial, and Hubert, of the Worcesters, has been killed in Italy The officer, whose sergeant he was, lost his life in the same action. The commanding Officer, in a sympathetic letter to the father says:- ``It was the fine spirit in which your son and his comrades followed their officers and non-commissioned officers which led to the success of the engagement. I, as his commanding officer, can say I have lost a brave man" A kindly-written letter from the Chaplain says:- ``Hubert died gallantly in a noble cause, and his body lies buried in the military cemetery on the Asiago Plateau, the grave being marked. Before joining up, Pte. Pugh was gardener to Mr. H. Basil Harrison, of Manor House, whose tribute one of which the father may well feel proud, Hubert Pugh had many friends in the town who deeply mourn his loss.

Sapper Thomas Pugh
Service No 165006
Age: 33
Gloucestershire Regiment. Died on 17th March 1917
at Willesden Hospital, London. Buried in Pershore
Cemetery
Son of Alfred & Jane Pugh of Church Row,
Pershore

Evesham Journal 21 March 1917 ``PERSHORE SOLDIER'S DEATH

Great sympathy is felt for Mrs. Pugh, of High-Street, Pershore, in the death of her husband, Sapper Thomas Pugh, of the Royal Engineers, which occurred at Willesden Hospital, London on Saturday. Deceased, who was 33 years of age, was the third son of Mr. Alfred Pugh, of the Newlands, and was worthy of the esteem in which he was generally regarded as that of a straightforward, manly young fellow.

He was a good footballer, and filled the position as right back in the local team for many years. He was also, as may not be generally known, quite skilled in the art of gymnastics. he was a bricklayer by trade, and before joining the Royal Engineers in May last year worked for Messrs. Nicholas Bros., and also other local firms. His brother Hubert (the youngest son of Mr. A. Pugh) is now lying wounded in the General Hospital at Edgbaston.

Mrs. T. Pugh is left with two young children. Her husband came scatheless through several engagements, but the rigours of trench warfare gave him pneumonia, which was the ultimate cause of his death. Mrs. Pugh was in the hospital when he passed away. His body was brought to Pershore on Wednesday, and was taken to the home for the night.

On Thursday, the Vicar (the Re. A. H. Philips conducted the burial service at the cemetery. The mourners were Mrs. T. Pugh (widow) Mr. and Mrs. Alfred Pugh (father and mother), Messrs. Fred Pugh and Arthur Pugh (brothers), Sapper T. Cornelius (Royal Engineers, brother-in-law) Floral tributes were sent by all members of the family, also Mr. and Mrs. G. Summers (a former employer), Mr. and Mrs. W. Winwood, Mr. and Mrs. Joynes, Mr. and Mrs. T. Cornelius, etc."

Private Charles J REEVES
Service No 19093
Age: 21
Sherwood Foresters 11th Battalion
Died of wounds on 6th October 1916 at Flanders
Listed on Sherwood Foresters Roll of Honour and on
The Thiepval Memorial, Somme, France.
Born in Pershore in 1895.
Lived at 14 Howard Road, Mansfield and enlisted at
Mansfield. Occupation in 1911 was Co-operative
Stable Boy.
Nephew of Harry & Emma Smith.

Private Robert REEVES
Service No 27664
Age: 35
Worcestershire Regiment 3rd Battalion
Killed in action at Flanders France on 24th August 1916
Commemorated at Lonsdale Cemetery, Authuile,

Somme, France
Son of Mrs Elizabeth Reeves of Priest Lane, Pershore

William James RICHARDS
Service No 59127
Age: 22
9th Div. Ammunition Col. Royal Field Artillery
Killed at Flanders France on 16th October 1917
Commemorated at Vlamertinghe New Military
Cemetery
Son of John & Annie Richards of Bearcroft,
Pershore

James Richards

Evesham Journal Nov 3rd 1917 -- ``PERSHORE MAN
KILLED.

_James Richards (Royal Field Artillery) eldest son of Mr. William
Richards, builder and contractor of Pershore, has been killed in France.
The Bereaved parents have received a very sympathetic letter from
Cpt.   Townshend, in which he said the young soldier was killed
instantly by a German shell, and this would be keenly felt by all ranks
of that section. Pte. Richards, who was 22 years of age, joined up in
the early part of 1915, and had experienced hard fighting in France. He
was one of the Pershore Company of Boy Scouts who attended the
King's Review in London a few years ago. His brother Albert Edward
[see above] was in the Gallipoli campaign, and is now in France.
(Thanks to Dave Brusselen for information, including photos, on the
above two Richards brothers)_

Corporal Thomas Lloyd ROPER
Service No 325529
Age: 20
1st/1st Queen's Own Worcestershire Hussars
(Worcester Yeomanry)
Died aged 20 on 31st July 1916 at Angora
Born Knightwick - enlisted in Worcester.
Buried in Baghdad (North Gate) War Cemetery,
Iraq, Angora Memorial 141 Appears on: Worcester Cathedral
Worcestershire Hussars,
& on Pershore Abbey memorial
Thomas & Fanny Roper of Huntly Villas, 31 Westcliffe Drive,

Blackpool Brother of Mrs Harris of Pinvin. Worked at Fish Shop.

T.L. Roper 1st/1st Worcester Yeomanry, 1st Draft, embarked at Devonport 23rd October 1915 for service with the Mediterranean Expeditionary Force, disembarked at Mudros 6th November 1915, disembarked at Alexandria, Egypt on 30th November 1915.

Trooper Maurice H SAUNDERS
Service No 3190
Age: 27
Worcester Yeomanry
Died on 14th November 1918 in Turkey.
Son of Henry & Caroline Saunders, Priest Lane, Pershore

Maurice Henry Saunders was born on 23rd January 1891 in Evesham, Worcestershire. He resided in Priest Lane, Pershore when he was appointed as Police Constable No 10, Worcester Constabulary on 23rd January 1914. He was single and his previous employment was with the Prudential Assurance Company in Pershore as an Insurance Agent. He was 6 feet, half an inch tall, weighed 12 stone 5lbs, his chest measurement was 36 inches and he had a fresh complexion with brown eyes and brown hair. He had a scar on the middle finger of his left hand. Maurice spent 246 days with the constabulary as a Constable 3rd Class, working at Police Headquarters in Worcester until 8th January 1915 and then at Stourport Police Station from 9th January 1915 where he remained until he left the police force to enlist in the army on 11th June 1915.

Listed as missing in Evesham Journal, 20 May 1916. Mentioned in a letter home from R.C. Edwards and printed in the Evesham Journal 29th December 1917 that mentions him amongst those captured by the Turks on Easter Sunday 1916, and still a prisoner in December 1917. Lived in Priest Lane

Evesham Journal July 8 1916:

Mrs. Saunders of Priest-lane, Pershore has had a letter from her son Trooper M.H. Saunders, in which he says that the prisoners are all being treated with the greatest kindness by the Turks and they are all in the best of spirits.

Evesham Journal February 8 1919:-- PERSHORE YEOMAN'S DEATH.

Official news has been received that Tpr. Maurice Saunders, of the Worcestershire Yeomanry, died on November 14 of malaria, at Niosibin, Turkey. Trooper Saunders, who was 28 years of age, joined the Yeomanry in June 1915, and was captured by the Turks on Easter Sunday 1916. He was a finely built young fellow, and previous to joining the army was in the Worcestershire Constabulary and was stationed at Stourport. Deep sympathy is felt for his parents, who have another son in the Air Force.

Second Mate John Critchley SMITH
Mercantile Marine S.S. "Mahratta."
Age: 30
Died on 4th January 1918
Buried in Port Said War Memorial Cemetery, Egypt,
Grave D. 1. Appears on:
Worcester Kings School WW1 Memorial

John C. Smith

Worcester Cathedral Cloister Windows Kings School
Wyre Piddle War Memorial, Pershore Abbey, Fladbury St John the Baptist Church under Wyre casualties with the additional information: 1918
Son of Arthur William and Minnie Smith, of The Square, Pershore; Husband of Kathleen Smith, of Wyre, Pershore, Worcestershire

Sec. Lieut., R. N. R. Born, June 1, 1887. Killed, January 4, 1918.

J. C. Smith was the eldest son of Mr. A W. Smith, of Pershore. He entered the School as a day boy from the Royal Grammar School in January, 1899, and left early in April, 1902, after 3 years only of School life. He always desired a sailor's life, and after serving his apprenticeship he rapidly rose in the Mercantile Marine. In his 15 years of seafaring life he made voyages to the West Indies, Costa Rica, New York, S. America and India. He obtained his Captains ticket three years since, and was recently married. Since the outbreak of war he has been engaged in the transport service, and was very popular with his fellow-officers. He was marvellously successful with his navigation, and had brought his boat safely through the Mediterranean at the end of last year, when he was killed by an accident at Port Said. He was one of those whom the Merchant Service can ill spare.

With grateful thanks to Remember The Fallen website.

(Second Officer) R.N.B. Eldest son of Arthur William Smith. Killed by an accident on Board his ship at Port Said January 4th 1918. Had his Captain's ticket 5 years - too young to be made a Captain.

Evesham Journal 16 February 1918 - DEATH OF 2nd OFFICER J. CRITCHLEY SMITH.

Particulars have now reached England of the death on January 5 of Second Officer J. Critchley Smith, eldest son of Mr. and Mrs. Arthur Smith, of Pershore. The agents of Messrs. Thos. & Jon. Brocklebank write from Port Said:-- ``The Mahratta was leaving her berth with engines going ahead when the stern rope jammed. Before way could be taken off the ship's rope parted and struck the second officer breaking both his legs and fracturing the base of his skull. The doctor of the Blue Funnel liner, Ning Chow, was promptly on the scene, and Dr. Wigham also sent for. Mr. Smith was brought ashore as soon as possible, but died on the way to the hospital from injuries received.

An inquiry was held at the Consulate the following day and he was buried that afternoon. The burial was attended by the officers and engineers of the Malakuta (another ship on which Mr. Smith had formerly served) and Mr. E.J. Williams represented us." Mr. Smith was born in Pershore on June 1 of the first Jubilee year and was educated at Hanley Castle School and King's School, Worcester. He served his apprentice with Messrs. Elders and Fyffe's, and in his fifteen years of sea-faring life made many voyages to the West Indies, Costa Rica, New York, South America, Australia, and India. He obtained his captain's ticket about three years ago and since the commencement of war had been engaged on transport service. He was very popular with his fellow officers and during his rare and brief holidays, his simple, unassuming manners and happy breezy disposition endeared him to very many in Pershore and Wyre. The greatest sympathy has been *shown to his young widow and to his parents and the other members of the family."*

Driver Henry (Harry) Silas Smith
Service No 246209
Age: 20
Royal Horse Artillery
Died on 16th February 1918
Buried in Pershore Cemetery
Son of John & Mary Smith of Newlands, Pershore

Evesham Journal 23rd February 1918 - *A SECOND SON KILLED*

Harry Smith

Mr. and Mrs. John Smith, of the Newlands, Pershore, whose eldest son, William, of the Worcesters, was killed in action last August, have now received the sorrowful news that their other soldier son, Gunner Harry Smith, of the Royal Horse Artillery, was killed by anti-aircraft guns in London on the 18th inst. The announcement was made by a telegram from the Colonel of the Regiment, and Inspector Pegg who received a message requesting him to see the bereaved parents and ask if they would care to attend the inquest at London on the 31st inst. Mr. and Mrs. Smith went up on Tuesday and returned on Thursday, bringing the body of their son with them for burial.

The late Harry Smith, who had not attained his twentieth birthday, joined the Army exactly three years ago. After his training he was sent to Egypt, and then to Salonika. While on his way home from the latter place in July last his ship was torpedoed and he was rescued after being six hours in the water. He was a few weeks in hospital. After this he came home on a short furlough last August Bank holiday week. Since then to the time of his death he was with his regiment in London. Before the war he and his late brother Pte. William Smith were employees of Mr. E.P. Whiteley, market gardener, of Pershore. The townspeople deeply sympathise with the parents in their double bereavement.

Evesham journal, 2 March 1918:-- PERSHORE SOLDIER KILLED IN AIR RAID.

The body of Gunner Harry Silas Smith, of the Royal Horse Artillery, who was killed during an air raid on London recently, was brought by his parents to Pershore on Thursday and buried at the Cemetery, the Rev. L. rivers-Tippett conducting the service. The father (Mr. John Smith) attended the inquest at London, and learnt that his son was making his way towards his barracks while the raid was in progress, and has stopped a few minutes to make a purchase at a fruiterer's shop, when a bomb fell on the premises burying him and a soldier companion beneath the debris. As stated last week, this is the second son Mr and Mrs Smith have lost, the eldest boy being killed in France six months ago. The parents have the sympathy of all in this painful bereavement. [list of those attending and floral tributes omitted here] The bearers were Pte. Jack Taylor, Lance corpl. Ralph Clark, Pte. W. Mumford, Pte. R.T. Smith

Private William John Smith (or John William Smith)
Service No 240804
``D" Company 8th (Res.) Worcesters
Killed in action at Flanders, France on 27th August
1917 aged 23.
Listed as John W. on Abbey Memorial.
Listed on the Tyne Cot memorial
Son of John and Mary Ann Smith of the Newlands

Evesham Journal 15th September 1917 in an article on Pershore casualties - ``The third soldier reported killed is Pte. Will Smith, eldest son of Mr. and Mrs. J. Smith of the Newlands. He was a Territorial. Lieut. Willis, in his touching letter of sympathy, speaks well of him as a soldier."

Private Percy W Smith
Service No 16560
Grenadier Guards Reserve Bn.
Died on 1st June 1915 in London
Hospital Buried at Brompton Cemetery, London
Son of Arthur & Mary Smith of Ganderton Row, Pershore
Evesham Journal 29th July 1916 recounts that Percy Smith had been a member of the Pershore Hockey Club. Evesham Journal 19 Feb 1916 recounts he

Pte. Percy W. Smith
(of Pershore).
Died of spotted fever.

died of a head wound, in a London hospital. Photo in Berrow's Journal (above) quotes Spotted Fever.

Evesham Journal 14th November 1914 - *PERSHORE POSTMAN'S EXPERIENCES Private Percy Smith of Pershore now lies wounded in the West Field Military Hospital at Aberdeen, Scotland from which place he has written to his parents telling them of the trying experiences through which he has passed. Private Percy Smith was but nineteen years of age when he joined the Grenadier Guards some sixteen months ago. He was a postman at Pershore and was also groundsman for the town Hockey Club.*

He writes "I have had a most trying time since I left England, the worst being after we landed at a place called Zeebruges in Belgium but I must not grumble for many of my pals will never write or see old England again. Out of my lot of 200 which went out, only 65 returned uninjured. I've got a bullet wound in the top of the head. It is very painful at times and gives me terrible headaches. At time the room where I am lying seems fairly dancing but thank God I am getting much better. I really thought my time had come. I waited three hours for death, for as I lay there the devils kept shelling us but at last somebody dragged me into a ditch and later on, by all accounts, they fetched me on a stretcher and took me into a barn where I lay expecting every minute to see the place blown away by shelling. The firing got too hot and the wounded had to be again removed. They took me away in a cart and all the way we were constantly being shelled. I really cannot account for being here for six of my pals have gone. Old Bill Kings seems to have been lucky. He and I were together all the time until I got bowled over. I tell you Mother, I could almost write a book on the close shaves I have had from death, but I don't feel up to writing; I go so giddy at times. Many say it isn't war - it's murder with the guns used nowadays. It's nothing to see a house blown clean away. The scenes are indescribable; beautiful houses and whole towns and villages on fire. I've seen some of our chaps cry at things done by the Uhlans and it makes me feel glad that I have been able to pull a few of them over. I suppose I shall be at it again in a short time. I think my rheumatics have quite gone, or I should bound to have felt them lately for we had to lie three nights and two days in the open trenches drenched to the skin and the cold was terrible. To warm us up we used to walk twenty miles a day. I've heard of folks walking in their sleep but fancy a battalion asleep. I'm sure I must have done and scores of fellows have said the same. When ten minutes rest was called it took more than ten minutes to wake us up. I must close for I am feeling quite dazed but I must tell you the folks at this hospital are grand and generous. A lot of visitors come and bring us things, cigarettes especially."

Private Harry STANTON
Service No 241798
Age: 20
Worcestershire Regiment 1/8th Battalion
Killed in action at Flanders, France on 24th April 1917
Commemorated on Thiepval Memorial, Somme
Son of Richard & Katherine Stanton of Newlands,
Pershore

Harry Stanton

Evesham Journal 16 June 1917 - ``PERSHORE MAN MISSING.

Mrs. Coombs, of the Newlands, Pershore, has received information that her brother, Pte. H. Stanton, of the Worcesters, is missing. Before joining the army twelve months ago, Pte. Stanton was in the employ of Mr. J. Smith, builder, Pershore. His brother-in-law, Pte. T. Robbins is at present in Netley Hospital, after serving at the Dardanelles and Mesopotamia."

Evesham Journal 9 February 1918 - ``MISSING, NOW REPORTED KILLED.

Mrs. J. Robbins, of the Newlands, Pershore, has now received information that her brother, Pte. Harry Stanton, who was reported missing on April 24 1917, was killed on or about that date. Before joining the Army, Pte. Stanton worked for Mr. J. Smith, builder, Pershore, and was very much liked by all who knew him. The late Pte. Stanton has a brother and two brothers-in-law serving. We shall give a photo of Pte. Stanton next week.

Private Charles Percival SURMAN
Service No 5806
Age: 42
Gloucestershire Regiment 1st Battalion
Killed in action at Flanders on 25th November 1916
Listed on Loos Memorial

Born at Fairview, Cheltenham.
Married in 1908 in Pershore
Husband of Annie Surman of Newlands, Pershore.

Lance Corporal William Alfred TAYLOR
Service No 240805
Age: 25
Worcestershire Regiment 1/8th Battalion "B" Coy
Killed at Flanders, France on 9th October 1917
Listed on Tyne Cot Memorial
Son of George & Annie Taylor of New Road,
Pershore

Lance Corporal Ralph TINSON
Service No 9751
Age: 29
Worcestershire Regiment
Killed at Flanders, France on 16th December 1917.
Buried at Ribecourt British Cemetery, Nord, France
Son of Mrs W Turvey of Broad Street, Pershore

Ralph Tinson

Evesham Journal 2nd February 1918 - ``ANOTHER PERSHORE
SOLDIER KILLED. We regret to announce the death of another
Pershore soldier in Corpl. R. Tinson, of the Worcesters, who was killed
in action on the 16th of December 1917. He served with his regiment in
India for seven years, and was on the Reserve two years. When the
present war broke out he was recalled to his regiment, but had to
undergo an operation in Birmingham Hospital. He was in the battles of
Loos, La Basee, Neuve Chapelle, Ypres, and on the Somme.
Deceased was a brave and gallant soldier, liked by his officers and
company, who will sadly miss him. Deep sympathy is felt for his
mother, Mrs. W. Turvey, of Broad-street, Pershore"*

Private John William TOWNEND
Service No 10363
Age: 30
South Staffordshire Regiment 7th Battalion. Killed in
action on 9th August 1915 at Gallipoli Commemorated
on the Hellas Memorial
Son of Henry & Elizabeth Townend of Pensham

Serjeant Charles Edmund TWIGG
Service No 19173
Age: 22
10th Battalion Worcestershire Regiment
Killed in action on 23rd July 1916 at Flanders
Buried in Warloy-Baillon Communal Cemetery Extension,
France, Grave V. C. 26.
Went out September 14th 1914.
Appears on: Pershore Abbey, Worcester Post Office
Wainwright Road
Son of Charles and Florence Twigg of Head Street, Pershore
Brother of Leonard

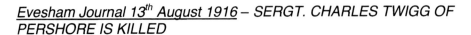

Evesham Journal 13th August 1916 – SERGT. CHARLES TWIGG OF
PERSHORE IS KILLED

Mr C Twigg, Auctioneer, of the Pershore Central Market has received
official notice that his eldest son, Sergt. Charles Twigg of the
Worcesters was killed in action on Sunday 2rd July. Sergt. Twigg, who
was but 22 years of age, had a host of friends in the Pershore district
who sincerely mourn his loss. Sergt. Twigg had been a long time in
hospital having been wounded and gassed in a previous engagement.
He had been in some very fine engagements since the July offensive
started. On 3rd July he sent his Father a letter saying that Will
Shepherd had been wounded and that Walter Aldington was now the
only chap he knew in his company. Sergt. Twigg joined up in
September 1914. Previous to that he was employed at Pershore Post
Office. He was a tall, nice looking lad and looked every inch a soldier.
He and his Brother Leonard, who is also in the army, were two of the
best footballers in the district and played for the Pershore Rovers, of
which club Charles was one time Captain."

Gunner Leonard TWIGG
Service No 81517
Age: 21
Royal Garrison Artillery 70th Siege Bty.
Killed in action at Flanders on 25th April 1918
Buried at Kelin-Vierstraat British Cemetery, Kemmel
Heuvelland, West-Vlaanderen, Belgium
Third son of Charles & Florence Twigg of Head St,
Pershore

<u>Evesham Journal, 11 May 1918</u>:-- *PERSHORE SOLDIER'S DEATH.*

There is a deep feeling of regret throughout Pershore at the death of Gunner Leonard Twigg, of the Royal Garrison Artillery, the second of the two handsome lads of Mr. Chas. Twigg of Head-street, who has fallen in the war. The eldest son, Charles, of the Worcesters, died from wounds received in action two years ago. From the letters received by Mr. Twigg, from the Major of the battery, Lieut. J.E. Stone, Battery Sergt.-Major R.L. Stone, and numerous comrades of the rank and file, it appears that Leonard was regarded as a very smart soldier, life popular with all, in death mourned by all. He was a signaller, and was out with other telephonists, including Lieut. Stone, on a reconnoitring expedition, when he was struck in the left side by a shell splinter and died instantaneously. Before joining up two years ago deceased worked at Pershore Post Office. Like his late brother Charles, deceased was a good sportsman, and was an idol in local football circles. It is a most painful bereavement for the father and sisters (the mother died two years ago) and great sympathy is felt for them.

Private William Charles WINWOOD
Service No 202003
Age:
8th Battalion Tank Corps. Killed in action at Cambrai on 1st December 1917 aged 21 Listed on Cambrai Memorial with no known grave Memorial on his parents' grave in Pershore Cemetery
Son of William & Agnes Winwood of Bridge St, Pershore

William Winwood

<u>Evesham Journal June 12 1915</u>:-- *A PERSHORE MAN'S WHIT MONDAY.*

A very interesting letter has been received from Gunner W. Winwood, of the 3rd. Batt. Motor Machine Guns, and son of Mr. W. Winwood, fruiterer, Bridge-street, Pershore. He says: ``I was just picturing the people enjoying themselves on Whit Monday, while we were wondering when we were going to get bowled over, but our luck was in, for we did not even get a casualty. It was my turn on the gun that day, and there was me laying under my bike and gun waiting for them to drop one on *me. But, thank God, it did not come off. The chap that was feeding the gun for me has been sent back to England with a nervous breakdown, So you can tell what it was like. That was in the morning. Then the enemy was not satisfied at that, they started sending shells over with the poisonous gases, and they dropped one right by the side of us, and then I did not remember any more until next morning when I found I was in a dressing station, where the doctor and two of our men had been giving me different kinds of medicine. The doctor said if I had been left another five minutes I should have been a `goner.' He also said I had a splendid constitution to have stood what I did. I shall never forget that Whit-Monday as long as I live. We are having beautiful weather. We are not wearing our shirts. We are stripped to the skin from morning until night. That was the 42nd. day in the fighting line without a rest."*

Evesham Journal, 1 June 1918:-- PERSHORE MAN PRESUMED KILLED. After six months' suspense, Mr. and Mrs. Winwood, of Bridge-street, have received an official letter from the War Office that it must be presumed that their son, Gunner William Charles Winwood, of the Tank Corps, at first reported missing, is killed. Gunner Winwood joined in September 1914, and was wounded in France the following June. He then sent home his battered cigarette case, which he was carrying in his breast pocket, and to which he attributed the saving of his life. After convalescence he was sent to Grantham, and was there employed for many months as dispatch rider. He was killed in the big fight of last December. An only child, a fine lad, his death is a hard trial for the father and mother. Sympathising letters have been sent by large numbers of residents, to whom they return grateful thanks.

Pershore's War Memorials
written by Marshall Wilson
(Re-printed with kind permission of his family)

In common with towns and villages across Britain, Pershore resolved to remember those who had served in the World War of 1914-1918. In September 1919, a Town Meeting resolved to form a committee to raise funds for the War Memorials. There were to be two Memorials, one for those who fell in the Great War and another to commemorate the war service of those who survived. There was general agreement that the Memorial to the Fallen should be placed in Pershore Abbey. The site decided upon was the centre of the South transept, the oldest part of the Abbey, already associated with the monuments of soldiers from other, older wars, including the knight of the thirteenth century. The preparation of the site required the repairs of the floor with large headstones taken from St Andrew's churchyard. The Victorian font had to be moved – it was sent to a church in Ceylon. This allowed for the return of the original Norman font from a garden in Kempsey!

As there were various opinions about the form of the Memorial, the committee sought the advice of Sir Aston Webb, the only architect ever to be elected President of the Royal Academy, the nephew of Mrs Hilditch Evans of Wick. He was connected with the Pershore churches for over forty years, having undertaken the 1887 restoration of St Andrew's. He recommended Alfred Drury, RA, as designer and sculptor. Alfred Drury was responsible for many war memorials including those at Malvern College and Kidderminster. His best-known work includes the bronze figures on the frontage of the Victoria and Albert Museum, the War Office and the statue of Sir Joshua Reynolds at the Royal Academy.

In his design, the figure of Immortality is represented as having just alighted on the terrestrial sphere, holding in her left hand the Olive Branch of peace. In her right hand she holds a Crown representing Everlasting Life. She stands on a pedestal of fine Portland stone. On the upper part of the front (North) of the pedestal is a bronze plaque depicting a fallen soldier with an angel on his head and his widow and child at the foot. Messrs Collins and Godfrey of Tewkesbury constructed the Memorial at a cost of £927.00.

Pershore sent one fifth of its adult population to the Great War. Of the 460 men who went, 101 (22%) never returned. Their names are recorded on the Memorial. They are listed without distinction of rank or title but simply alphabetically by the 26 Regiments and Services in which they served.

The War Memorial to the Fallen was dedicated at a moving Service on 1st November 1921. The Earl of Coventry, Lord-Lieutenant of the County, unveiled the Memorial. General Francis Davies of Elmley Castle, Officer Commanding Scottish Command, gave the Address.
The Memorial to the Living took the form of a Memorial Hall at a cost of £1,318.00. This extension to the Working Men's Club in the High Street enabled an amalgamation of that Club with the Old Comrade's Association. In February 1922, General Francis Davies unveiled a Memorial Board to the 63 former pupils who had attended the National School and who fell in the War. This board was moved to the Working Men's Club when the school in Defford Road was closed and demolished.

Twenty-three names of those from Pershore who fell in the 1939-1945 War were added to the board. On Remembrance Day 1950, General Sir Richard Gale, late of the Worcestershire Regiment and Commander of the Airborne Forces who landed on D-Day, unveiled these new names. One additional name was added, later. As a Town Memorial, a clock was erected on the Rural District Council Offices at 37 High Street.

The Memorial's own inscription sums up its spirit:

REMEMBER WITH THANKSGIVING THE TRUE AND
FAITHFUL MEN WHO IN THESE YEARS OF WAR
WENT FORTH FROM THIS PLACE FOR GOD AND THE RIGHT.
THE NAMES OF THOSE WHO RETURNED NOT AGAIN
ARE HERE INSCRIBED TO BE HONOURED FOR EVERMORE.
R.I.P.

In January 2011, Pershore & District Royal Naval Association paid £8,000 to Wychavon District Council for the construction of a new memorial stone and Garden at the entrance to the Abbey Park. The stone was quarried from Broadway is of the same Cotswold Limestone used to build Pershore Abbey. On Sunday 8th May 2011 at 3 p.m., the official opening of

the new Pershore Commemorative Garden was held and it was formally blessed and dedicated to honour all those men and women from the Town who have served their country in the Armed Forces. It was aptly timed as the last serving Tommy of WW1, Claude Choules (born in Bridge Street Pershore), died on 6th May 2011. A wreath was laid by the Lord Lieutenant of Worcestershire Michael Brinton and an Anchor wreath dedicated to Claude Choules was laid by the Mayor of Pershore, Councillor Chris Parsons. The Garden itself was designed by Wychavon Parks Officer Lynn Stevens and Trudy Burge of Pershore RNA.

The three Town Clocks

THIS CLOCK WAS ERECTED BY
PERSHORE TOWN COUNCIL
AND DEDICATED ON 28TH JUNE 2009
AS A REPLACEMENT FOR CLOCKS
INSTALLED IN 1953 AND 1973

IN MEMORY OF THOSE WHO GAVE THEIR LIVES
IN THE SECOND WORLD WAR

AND ALSO TO COMMEMORATE
THE SILVER JUBILEE OF HER MAJESTY
QUEEN ELIZABETH II

Those who survived ...

AB] Pershore Abbey War Memorial(listing those who died)
[AL] listed in Pershore Almanac,1915 edition i.e. a list of those who were in service around Dec 1914 or so.
[AV19] Absent Voters list for spring 1919
[EJXXXXXX] Evesham Journal Roll of Service - those listed as in service on a particular date
[EJD16] Evesham Journal, 8 Jan 1916 - Listing of the dead for the previous year

Sergt.-Major Walter Adams   Royal Artillery [AL] (tobacconist, High street, according to 1914 directory)

George Ryland Addis Lived in Bridge Street [AV18]

Private 19172 Walter Francis Aldington   Only son of Walter Aldington. Working for J.G. Baker. Kitchener's Army, then 10th Battn. Worcestershire Regiment Transp. Sect.: see the letter home written by Charles Twigg. Lived in No Gains 18. Joined up   July 1915, demobilised July 1919 [EJ140926][AL][AV18][AV19][SB]

3273 James L. Amos Royal Navy. Lived Church Row [AV19][SB]

Alfred Amphlett   Head Street. 2nd Worcesters. Father of Timothy George. Discharge 8 June 1926

Sergt. Alfred Amphlett   8th Worcesters [AL] Lived in Head Street.

Gnr. 120759 Timothy George Amphlett R.G.A. Son of Alfred. Lived in Head Street. Went out 21st September 1918 [AV18][AV19][SB]

Gnr. 23442 William Ernest Amphlett   R.F.A. Lived in New Road [AV18][AV19][SB]SB says R.G.A,

William George Amphlett Bull Entry. R.F.A. and R.A.S.C.   Went to France 24th December 1915, discharged 10th October 1917. [SB]

Sgt. 24023 Arthur Charles Andrews   52 Bat. Hants. Lived in High Street [AV18][AV19][SB]

2nd. Lieut. Charles Leslie Andrews   7th Worcesters. Lived in Newlands [AV18][AV19]

Cpl. 240307 Frank Andrews 2/8th Worcs. Regt. Lived in Head Street. Brother of George Sidney. Went out September 1914 [EJ141003][AL][AV18][AV19][SB] Ref. AL lists him as a private in Kitchener's army, which fits when he went out.

Private George Sidney Andrews   Territorials/ 1/8th Worcesters. Lived in Head Street. Joined up April 1914 [EJ140926][AL][AV18][SB]

Sergt. John Sidney Andrews R.A.F. Lived in Newlands([SB] says Post Office House) Second son of Holland Andrews, Driffield East Yorks. Obtained Commission in Sept 1918 [AV18][AV19][SB]

Leslie Charles Andrews 1/7th Worcs. Regt. Elder Brother of John Sidney. Italian Expeditionary Force, went out 23rd September 1917. [SB]

Albert Harry Annis   Service No: 263091 Worcestershire Regiment. Lived in Newlands [AV18] Son of Solomon Annis & Sarah Ann Annis (nee Houghton). Married Doris Hall in 1919.

Arthur Percival Annis *(see photo)* was born and bred in Pershore and lived in Birmingham Rd. Fortunately, he was one of the lucky ones who returned home and went on to live until the grand old age of 92.

Private 36180 Edward Annis 327 Co. Royal Defence Corps .Lived in Ganderton's Row [AV19] Occupation: Gardener. Married Rose Holland in Evesham in July 1891. Father to Ellen, Elsie, Edward & Florence.

James Annis Church Row [AV18]

James Annis Priest Lane [AV18]

Pte. 3705 (Christopher) Leonard Annis *(See photo)* 8th Worcs. Lived at 1, Church row [AV18][AV19]

Service No: 135708 Samuel Annis Royal Engineers - joined in October 1915. Lived in Head Street, married to Florence in 1911. Father of Margaret, Eleanor & George. Son of Reuben & Ann Annis.

Private 653978 William James Annis A.E. Worcestershire Regiment. Co. Labour Corps [AV18][AV19] Service Nos 557 & 658978. Married Florence Nellie Taylor in 1910. Iron moulder by trade. Lived in Victoria Terrace. Son of Solomon Annis & Sarah Ann Annis nee Houghton.

Private 30280 William James Annis *(see photo)* 11th Worcestershire Regiment. Lived at 3 Little Priest Lane [AV18][AV19] Joined up age 32 on 29th May 1916 and served until 16th February 1919. Height 5'4 ¾", Chest 35". Labourer by occupation. Son of James & Jane Annis of Priest Lane, Pershore. Married Frances Louisa Fletcher in 1906. Son William (Bill) and daughter Frances (Cis) later to be Neale. Widowed in 1921 and married Mary Edginton in 1931 And moved to Engine Terrace. Died 28th May 1949.

William James Annis 1/8th Worcesters. Brother of Arthur and James Samuel. In Italy. Went out August 1915. Demobilised July 1919. [SB]

Dr. Hugh Lowrie Askham *(See Photo)* Royal Army Medical Corps, according to the Evesham Journal 29 July 1916, which mentions that he'd been a member of the Pershore hockey club. Lived in Bridge street. An Evesham Journal story (28 April 1917) about his partner, Dr. H.B. Emerson (see that entry) mentions that he had returned home after a year's hard work in France. Evesham Journal 16th February 1918 has a report of his wedding, and a photo of him and his bride in the following issue. [SB]

Private John Baker 8th Worcesters [AL][EJ140926]

Lieut. John Herbert Baker 112 Siege Battery. Only son of J.G. Baker, Maltster, Bridge Street. Went out Christmas Day 1916. Demobilised at Gloucester. Evesham Journal, Feb. 2 1918 mentions that Mr. John

Griffin Baker of Bridge Street was ill; his son Lieut. John H Baker is now home on leave from France

Dvr. 86773 Cyril Uris Ball 116 Batty., Royal Field Artillery. Lived at top of Newlands. Went out March 1915. [AV18][AV19][SB]

William Izor Ball 2nd Worcesters. Brother of Cyril. Went out July 1916. [SB]

Charles Ballinger 2/5th Gloucesters. Lived in Church Street. [AV18] In Huddersfield. March 1917. Demobilised [SB]

Pte. 240803 Harry Ballinger 9th Worcs. Lived in Church Street. Went out in 1914. Demobilised. [AV18][AV19][SB]

Private Henry Ballinger 8th (Res) Worcs. Regt. - had served in S. Africa [EJ141003][AL]

41735 John Wicketts Ballinger Company Q.M.Sergeant, King's Liverpool Regiment. Lived in Whitcroft. Went out November 1917. Suffered a poisoned foot April 1918 [AV18][AV19][SB]

Cpt. 29553 Ralph Ballinger MC 4th Battn. Surrey Regt. Lived at Whitcroft. Brother of Walter and John Wicketts. Went out Oct. 1917. Was at Hanson's. Won the M.C. in September 1918. All his Officers and N.C.C.s were killed- he brought back his company safely. [AV18][AV19][SB] says 12th Gloucesters.

L-Cpl 231785 Walter Ballinger R.E. Brother of John Wicketts. Lived at Whitcroft [AV18][AV19][SB] says Not out: at Chatham,

Private William "Willie" Ballinger 8th Worcesters. Lived at Church Street. Went out with Territorials. In Devon. Demobilised. [AL][AV18][SB]

Harold Barber 10th Worcesters. Lived in Priest lane. Cousin of William and Annie Barber (now Reynolds) of Priest Lane. Wounded in his hand [SB][AV18]

Evesham Journal, 27 April 1918:-- PERSHORE MAN A PRISONER.

Mrs. Harold Barber, of Priest-lane, Pershore, has received news that her husband, Pte. H. Barber, of the Worcesters, was recently severely wounded and is now in Hospital at Leicester. Pte. Barber was gassed in July, and only returned to France three weeks ago. Prior to joining up he worked at the Pershore Post Office as rural postman. He has two other brothers with the colours, Driver J. Barber, now in Italy, and Pte. V.C. Barber in France.

157792 Henry William Barber Lived in Church Street. Lance Corporal 2nd Hampshires, no 42246. Went out Dec 5th 1917. Wounded. 2nd Batt. M.G.C. 1918, [AV18][AV19][SB]

Private Victor C. Barber 8th Worcesters. Was in France in April 1918. see Harold Barber entry above. [AL]

Private Edward Barnard National Reserve (Railway Guard) [AL] Church Street.

Alfred Barnes Served. Lived in Newlands. [AV18][SB] No other information.

Pte. Alfred Barnes Garr. Bn. Northants. Newlands. [SB] No other information.

Ralph Bateman No other information [SB]

Private Ernest Batty No-Gains. Son of George Batty (Big Drum man). 2/8th Worcesters Went out May 1918.[AL][SB]

George Robert Batty Nogains. 1/38 London Artists' Rifles. Brother of Ernest. Went out 1st April 1918. [SB]

Bombardier 305020 George Robert Batty Father of the two brothers named above. Lived in No Gains. Royal Field Artillery. At Portsmouth guarding the bridge at entrance. Went up 1914.[AL][AV18][AV19][SB]

Private 35337 Francis William Baylis ('Frank') 9th Worcesters. Mesopotamia. Went out Dec 1916. Brother of Charles Henry. Lived in Broad Street In August 1917 was serving in India: before the war had been with Messrs. Phillips and Sons of Pershore - see his brother

Harry's entry below. [AV18][AV19][SB] AV18 spells his name with two `s's.

Gerald Baylis Gloucester Cycle Corps, discharged as medically unfit not long before August 1917 - see the entry for his brother Harry.

Rifleman R/4194 Charles Henry Baylis ('Harry')
(See Photo) Telephone Office, Pershore. 2nd King's Royal Rifles. Lived in Broad Street. Garr. Bn. Northants. Newlands. [SB] No other information.

Evesham Journal 4 August 1917:-- PERSHORE MAN MISSING.

Mrs. Bayliss, of the National telephone Office Pershore, has received information from the War Office that her son Harry, of the King's Royal Rifles, is missing. It is a terribly anxious time for her, as he was in the awful Flanders battle of July 10, at which the King's Royal rifles and Northamptons won imperishable fame for their valour and fidelity against impossible odds. Rifleman Harry Bayliss has been two years in France and has been through many big fights. When on short sick leave about a year ago, he brought home a Hun helmet, which is now in his mother's possession. Prior to the war, Harry was at the Union Club, Trafalgar-square, London. Mrs. Baylis has another son, Frank, in India with the colours. Formerly he was with Messrs. Phillis and Sons, Pershore. A third son, Gerald, of the Gloucester Cycle Corps, has been recently discharged as medically unfit.

Evesham Journal 22 September 1917:-- A PRISONER IN GERMANY.

To her great relief Mrs. Baylis, of the Telephone Office, Pershore, has received news of her son, Rifleman Harry Baylis, of the King's Royal rifles, who was reported by the War Office as missing since the sharp engagement at Nieuport on July 10, when his battalion, with the Northamptons. fought heroically against an overwhelming number of the enemy and suffered severe losses. Harry has sent two postcards to his mother, the first dated July 13, apprising her of his captivity, and the second the 14th of August, telling her he was all right, but would like `something to eat' sent on. Both cards were received this week, the last dated coming to hand first. Many Pershore people will share in Mrs.

Baylis's pleasure that her worst fears have proved unfounded. (rest of item continued under Arthur Hall)

Private Alfred James Beard   8th (Home Service) Batt. Worcs. Regt. Lived in Newlands, his father was Sam Beard of Ganderton's Entry. Joined up in 1914. Went first to France then to Italy Xmas 1917, then back to France Oct 1918. Wounded Oct 22nd 1918 -- his first injury during the war. [EJ141024][AL][AV18][SB]

Harry Beard   Noel Hill, Birmingham. Tank Corps.   Brother of Alfred James. In France. Joined up in 1914. Was in Territorials and went out a fortnight after war was declared. [SB]

204073 Harry James Beard 52nd West Yorks. Lived in Church Street [AV18][AV19]

Private Henry Beard   Labour Company. South African War [SB]

Private Henry Beard   National Reserve (Railway Guard) Lived at Newlands [AL][AV18]

Pte. 227750 Thomas Beard   Labour Batt. Lived at Plough Lane (SB says Priest Lane) [AV18][AV19][SB] Probably the Pte. T. Beard attending at Harry Smith's funeral in early 1918.

Lance Corporal 9280 William Beard   2nd Battalion Worcester Regiment. Born in Pershore, enlisted at Worcester (living at Henley-in-Arden, Warks. at the time) Served in France and Flanders. Killed in action 26th September 1915

Pte. Arthur Oswald Bell   M.T.A.S.C. Brother of James Edward and Thomas. In Salonica, April 1918, contracted Malarial fever. Grimley, near Worcester [SB

Corpl. James Edward Bell   of Cropthorne. 2nd Oxford & Bucks. L.I. Son of Widow Bell, Newlands. Served over two years from 1916. Gassed March 15th 1918 [SB]

Pte. Thomas Bell 2nd Worcesters. Brother of James Edward. Lived in Plough Lane.   Listed in 1915 Pershore Almanac as Wounded   and taken Prisoner of War.[SB] says he was taken prisoner Oct 21st 1914. Had nearly 10 years of service. [AL][AV18]

Pte. 550007 William George Bell 6th Worcesters. Brother of above three. Lived in Newlands. In hospital in Essex. Wounded May 22nd 1917. Joined up in 1915 [AV18][AV19][SB]

Lieut-Col. C.H. Bennett, D.S.O. 3rd Batt. P.S.U., Brigade [AL] Manor House, Bridge Street.

Hubert Berry Pensham [AV18]

Sidney Berry Pensham [AV18]

Albert Cyril Beynon High Street, Pershore. 98th Infantry, Indian Army. Youngest son of Mr & Mrs A.E. Beynon. Went out Dec 1 1916. In Egypt. Was 2nd Lieut in 14th Cheshires. [SB]

Pte. 38603 Frederick Thomas Bick Qr. 9th Royal Nth. Lancashires Musketry School, France. Dec 1917. Brother of Harry. Lived in Binholme [AV18][AV19][SB]

Lance-Corporal 7371 Harry Bick 15th King's Hussars. 9th Cav Brigade. 1st Cav. Division. Lived in Binholme. France. Went out August 9 1914 [AL][AV18][AV19][SD] [AL] lists him as private.

Private 240500 Joseph William Surman Bick 8th Worcs. Brother of Harry. Lived in Binholme. In Italy. Went out April 1914 [AL][AV18][AV19][SB]

Private 25772 Arthur James Bickerstaff A Squadron, R.R.E. Lived in Bridge Street [AV18][AV19]

Private 035716 Emmanuel Blackwell Army Ordnance Corps. [AV18][AV19] Lived High Street, Plough Inn. October 24th 1915 [AV18][AV19][SB]

Trooper T. Blizzard Worcester Yeomen - listed as missing in Evesham Journal, 20 May 1916
Arnold Irving Henry William Bloxham Operator, Wireless Staff, Marconi Company. Lived in Bridge Street [AV18][AV19]

Trooper Alfred James Boswell Worcester Yeomen - listed as Missing in Evesham Journal, 20 May 1916; evidently still alive for his listing in ref. [AV18]

44007 Charles William Stanley Boulter Berkshire Regiment. Born abt 1899 in Wyre. Supposedly living at Allesborough Cottages, Pershore by the time of the war according to [AV18][AV19], though when he signed up, age 17 on 22 Oct 1917, his sign up papers recorded his address as Lower Moor.

15386 Harry Victor Boulter 1st Worcesters. Born in Wyre like his brother Charles above. Lived at Allesborough Cottages [AV19]

14964 George Bourne Royal Marines. Lived in Priest Lane [AV18][AV19][SB]

George William Thomas Bozzard DCM Private 20027 5/Shrops Light Infantry, then Lance Corporal 44504 Somerset Light Infantry. Brother of Arthur above. Lived in High Street. Fought in France, went out 24 November 1915. Awarded the Distinguished Conduct Medal, 24th Oct 1918. [AV18][SB]

C. Bradstock Batchelor's Entry. Wounded. No other information [SB]

Private Edward Brant Kitchener's Army [AL]

Edward George Brant Brother of Alfred. 5th Worcesters. Gassed and Wounded. Discharge October 1915 [SB]

41119 Ernest Brant Royal Irish Rifles. Lived in Newlands. [Av19]

Private Ernest Brant 8th Hussars. Lived in Newlands, opposite Champkens. Wounded, went to Southampton. Discharged July 27th 1918 [AL][AV18][SB]

G. Brant Kitchener's Army [EJ140926]

Jack Brant 23583. 11th Worcesters, France. Brother of Mrs. Fulcher. [SB]

Jack Brant [SB]

Private 23583 John Reginald Brant ('Jack') Lived in Newlands. Went out 1915 to Dardenelles [AL][AV18][AV19][SB][AL] lists him in Kitchener's Army, [AV19] has him in the 11 Hants One entry in SB says 3rd Hampshires, [another entry there says 11th Worcesters!. His sister was Mrs A.E. Fulcher

Arthur Brewer Lived at The Abbey [AV18]

William Peake Brown Pte. Lab. Coy. Lived in Newlands [AV18][SB]

Dr Gordon Browning Royal Navy, according to Evesham Journal 29 July 1916 which says he'd been a member of Pershore's hockey club: SB says he was a Lieut. in R.A.M.C.

Private George Charles Buckle 8th/9th Worcesters. Son of the late Mr and Mrs Buckle of Pershore. In Mesopotamia. Went out 1914.[SB]

Evesham Journal, 27 May 1916 - ` ``ALL GOOD BOYS IN THE WORCESTERS"_

Pte. G.C. Buckle, who has been wounded and is at present on a hospital ship, writing to his sister, Mrs. Green, of 12, Bourne's-place, says ``Just a few lines to let you know that I am going on well now. My wound is healing up, and I have very little pain so that I think I shall soon be able to get up and about again. I was wounded on the 5th of April, 1916 when in the attack. We were to take three lines, but of course we were so eager to get them out, that we all pressed forward and cleared the Turks out of their possession, and got them on the run. I got hit when I was getting into the fourth trench.

I daresay you will like to know whether I got the box of fags, I got them just before I went into action. I had only one and then put the rest in my haversack, and when I got hit I had to leave everything behind me. I had not had a smoke for three days, so I could have stopped and had a good smoke. I clung to your photos of you and the children, but lost everything else. I have been sent to India now so I do not know when I shall get back to dear old England. I am going all over the world, am I not? Our General saw me when I was coming down to the dressing station, and he cheered me up a bit, and put his hand on my shoulder and said, we were all good boys in the Worcesters, and we had done very well. He is very proud of his lads and we of him, for he is a good old sort. My chum told me there was a letter for me about three minutes before we had to go into action, but there was not time to get it. It's hard lines when one gets one's letters so near as that and then can't have them. I have still got the bullet in my throat, but shall have it out very soon now, I hope"

Sergeant Joseph Buckle *(See photo)*
Motor Transport Army Service Corps. Brother of Arthur Buckle. Joined August 1914. Discharged 22nd November 1917. [SB] Son of the late Mr and Mrs. Buckle of Pershore, had enlisted at the beginning of the war - Evesham Journal 27th May 1916.

J. Buckle

Evesham Journal, 15 May 1915:-- *THANKS TO EVESHAM LADIES*

.

Pte. J. Buckle, of the M.T.A.S.C., Meerut Divisional Train, Indian Expeditionary Force, writing to his sister, Mrs. G. Green, of Borthwick-terrace, Evesham, thanks her for her letter and glorious parcel which he had just received and also one from ``the kind ladies you asked to help us out here, Mrs. Smith and Mrs. Bell. Thanking them and you again and again for all you have done while we have been out here. I am sure it has all been most thankfully received. I have been feeling very queer lately, but am much better now, thank Good. We have been through something this winter. It has been hell upon earth out here. I have been all over the country since I wrote to you first. I was very sorry to hear the sad news of my brother, Will, being wounded, as I was with him only a day or two before he was hurt. I hope he will soon recover, but I think as he has received four bullets poor chap; he is one of the lucky ones to escape with that, but his time was not come, was it? He might have been killed and I too, for look at the months we have been out here. Give him my love when you write to him at Netley and tell him I will write. I shall be glad when it's all over, I tell you, if only for a good rest. Fancy Easter has come and gone and we did not know out here till we received our Easter cards and greetings from home. I have not seen G. Clifton, Dennick or W. Coombes during the last few days, but they are here somewhere."

AT NEUVE CHAPPELLE. In a letter written on April 28, Pte. Buckle tells his sister that he is getting better and thanks her for her latters and *paper. He proceeds:-- ``As you say it is dreadful to read the papers, but it is more dreadful to be here. You say you are pleased I was not in the Hill 60 affair, but we happened to be in the same village, Neuve Chapelle. That was horrible. At the same time we had to force the Germans out from Hill 60. I am glad to hear poor Will is getting better. Since I started writing this letter I have more news to tell you. I and my car have been 3 ½ hours under most terrific German shell fire at Ypres. The place is all ablaze; a most shocking sight. I never saw such a sight and hope I never shall again. I am pleased to say I got my car away in safety.*

I was with my car watching the shells bursting about twenty to fifty yards away when one shell came right into the house only two yards where I and my car and officers were. You may guess it was a very hot shop to be in. The shells were bursting everywhere so we did not know where to go for safety."

THE BUCKLE FAMILY.

The Buckle family, of Pershore, is doing its part in the war, and we give portraits of four brothers, sons of the late Mr. and Mrs. Buckle, of Pershore, their brother-in-law, and the brother-in-law's brother, who are all serving. Lance-Corpl. William Buckle, of the 1st Worcesters, is an old soldier and fought through the South African War. He has recently been discharged owing to wounds received at Neuve Chapelle. Sergt. J. Buckle, of the Motor Transport A.S.C., enlisted at the commencement of the war; Pte. Arthur Buckle, of the 4th Worcesters, has seen a lot of fighting in more than one theatre of war, and Pte. G. C. Buckle, of the 8th Worcesters, was wounded on April 5 in one of the distant theatres. He is now convalescent. Driver G. Green, of the Army Service Corps, married the sister of these soldier brothers, and his brother, Pte. Edgar Green, is in the 1st Worcesters.

Evesham Journal article about the Buckle family

Lance Corporal William Buckle *(see photo)* 1st Worcesters. Son of the late Mr and Mrs Buckle of Pershore. Had fought in the South African War. Had recently been discharged owing to wounds received at Neuve Chappell. - Evesham Journal 27 May 1916.

William Buckle

James Bunday Lun's Yard. Worcesters. R.E. Son of Mrs Perry of Bearcroft Cottages. Married the housemaid from Lower Hill in 1916. Discharged Oct. 1916 with severe shell shock. [SB]

Alfred Burnham Lived in Bridge Street [AV18]

Sapper 552593 Arthur Burton Royal Engineers. Lived Rose Cottage, New Road [AV18][AV19][SB]

Sapper 23532 Frank Martin Stone Butt Royal Engineers. Lived High Street [AV18][AV19][SB]

J. Caldrick Territorials [EJ140926]

Aircraftsman 1st Class Robert William Camden -
Service No 142053. Robert served n the RAF and he joined about 3 weeks after his 18th birthday on 12 April 1918. He was posted to the British Expeditionary Force and AD aircraft depot in France He was then transferred to 12 Squadron until 13th October 1919 having been

appointed Aircraftsman 1st class. Commemorated on Wyre Piddle War Memorial. Robert was the son of Benjamin and Amy Camden of Wyre Piddle. He married Beatrice Teague in 1922 in Pershore. He died in 1937.

Charles Catlin Son of Mr. & Mrs. F. Catlin of Pensham, was serving in Royal Navy in June 1917 (see entry below for his brother Fred Catlin)

Private 14051 Edgar John Catlin 2nd. Coldstream Guards. Lived in Pensham [AV18][AV19] Son of Mr. & Mrs. F. Catlin of Pensham. Was serving in France in June 1917 [see following entry for brother Fred]

Private Fred Catlin Worcestershire Regiment (listed as being in Kitchener's Army in [EJ140926])
Evesham Journal 4 June 1917 - ``WOUNDED IN SALONIKA*

Mr. and Mrs. F. Catlin, of Pensham, has been informed officially that their son, Pte. Fred Catlin, of the Worcesters, is wounded and is in the British Red Cross Hospital at Salonika. Pte. F. Catlin has been in the army some two years, and has fought against both the Germans in France and the Turks in Mesopotamia. Mr. and Mrs. Catlin have two other sons in the service, Edgar, now in the Coldstream Guards in

France, and Charles, in the Royal Navy, a typical British Tar, who has been in more than one scrap with German ships."

Private 246327 Lees Challenor 609 Ag. Co. Labour Corps. Lived at Manor Cottages [AV18][AV19]

Private Albert Champken 8th Worcesters [AL]
Evesham Journal 12 June 1915:-- PERSHORE MAN WOUNDED. Mrs. A. Champken, of Priest-lane, Pershore, has received notification that her husband, Pte. A. Champken was wounded on May 30. The wound is in the left shoulder, and he has been sent in to the base hospital. He is serving with the 8th Worcesters.

Private Henry Champken 8th (Home Service) Batt. Worcs. Regt. [AL][EJ141024] N.B:- EJ reference spells his name as ``Champkins"

Private H/325722 Jim Champken Worcester Yeomanry. Lived at Talbot Inn [AV18][AV19]

Private William Champken 8th Hussars [AL]

Fred Charlwood 188 Batt., Canadian Buffs. Was paper boy and in printing office at Smith's, Bridge Street. Joined up 1918. Brother of Frank. [SB]

Corporal 1514 William Frank Checketts 1st/8th Worcestershire Regiment. Son of Mr and Mrs. H. Checketts of Head St. Pershore. [EJ140926][AL] NB. Ref AL listed him as a private; he was a Corporal in the Territorials, and saw action until 1916; he was released for important war work but later recalled into the royal Berkshire Regt. (Private 43100) until the end of the war. One source says the 1st, [AV18][AV19] say it was the 5th Royal Berkshire. Lived in Head Street His health broken by his experiences, he died 3rd July 1920 age 25. Buried in Pershore Cemetery 14th July 1920.[EJ140926][AL] [AV18][AV19][AB]

Sapper Arthur William Chick Royal Engineers, Postal Section. Son of Chick, old Postman, last house in Bridge Street. Went to Italy February 11 1918. Went to France 3rd April 1918. [SB]

C. Chubb Kitchener's Army [EJ140926]

James Clarke Lived in Head Street [AV18]

Private Frederick Clarke 8th Worcesters [AL][EJ140926]

Sergeant 202901 Frederick John Clarke R. Warwicks. Lived in Victoria Terrace [AV18][AV19]

Lance-Corporal Ralph Edward Clarke Lived in Head Street [AV18] Was apparently one of the bearers at Harry Smith's funeral, early 1918: his rank was listed there as Lance-corpl.

Ralph Henry Clarke 10th Worcesters. Head Street. Joined up 7th June 1915. Married Lizzie Robbins. [SB]

Charles Clemens No other information. [SB]

Private George Clifton King's Royal Rifles [AL]

Evesham Journal 31 July 1915:-- PERSHORE MAN HOME.

Pte. George Clifton, one of the several soldier sons of Mr. Samuel Clifton, of The Newlands, has just returned to the front after six days' furlough. His home-coming was opportune, though rather sad, for his father is very old and lies seriously ill. Pte. G. Clifton is a splendid type of the British `Tommy'; he seems built just the right way for hard campaigning. He was a reservist in the Royal Rifles and went all through the Boer War without a scratch. He went out with the first Expeditionary Force, and says he shall never forget the wonderful welcome given the Army by the people of France - especially the ladies. His regiment, he says, came off remarkably light in the great retreat from Mons, but have had its full share of death and glory in the subsequent battles of the Aisne, Marne, Soissons and Cateau. He has as yet come through safely, but says that no less than seven times comrades fighting each side of him have been killed, and once he had a marvellous escape only three weeks ago. He brought a wounded pal from the firing line to the dressing station, laid him on the ground and covered him with a coat till the doctor could attend to him. He then went to fetch him some water. He was not more than three minutes away, but when he came back he was shocked to see that a shell had dropped right on the poor fellow and nothing was there but a few shreds of clothing and a hole in the ground. He says he has helped to dig out several `Jack Johnsons' and it takes five men to lift the exploded shell. Speaking of Mons - and it still remains the outstanding fight of the war - he says his regiment, except, perhaps, the officers, were positively not aware that the actual turning movement had taken place, and that it was the Germans who were retreating until one man noticed that the sun one morning was shining on their right, instead of on their left as before. Soldiers actually cried for joy on learning the truth. Just at that time he says they were hedged about with spies, and relates one instance of the penalty suffered by two of them. An old man, who affected a very simple manner, and his son, had followed their regiment for weeks selling cakes and sweetmeats. They were popular with the men but they asked so many questions as to the movements of the troops that the suspicions of an officer who overheard the boy one morning were aroused and they were closely watched. Proof was soon forthcoming of their traitorous conduct, and he, Pte. Clifton, was one of the squad that had to carry out the death sentence. As hard a soldier as he is, Pte. Clifton could not speak of the awful losses his gallant Royal Rifles have suffered without a trace of feeling. The battalion went out thirty over strength and on the last roll call just before he left only 40 of the rank and file and one officer - the old Colonel - were left to respond. They have lost, he says, over 200 officers and 3,000 casualties rank and file. His trench, he says, is only 22 yards from the German trench, and the feeling that it might at any time be blown up is not comfortable. A change is noticeable among the Germans, the biggest proof being in the ever-increasing number that steal away when the slightest opportunity occur and surrender. The Saxons are the best liked, the Prussians, Bavarians, and Wurtemburgers keep up their old hatred. He had no idea when the war would be over; they in the trenches knew really very little. Any big event happening in any other theatre of the war was posted up in the trenches.

Private Thomas Clifton   King's Royal Rifles [AL]

Private William Clifton   Army Service Corps [AL]

Capt. Neville Eden Cobbold   159 Labour Coy. Lived in High Street [AV18][AV19]

George Henry Coldicott   Lived in Broad Street [AV18]

Harry Coldicott Son of ``Bussie'' Coldicott, Broad Street. Joined up 1916. Royal Field Artillery: it's mentioned in his brother Albert's obituary (See above) that he was serving at the front in November 1916. [SB]

† **Private William Coldicott** Warwicks, died in training, sometime before Jan 1916. Source: [EJD16], though this ref spells his name as Caldicott

A. Cole Territorials: he is named in the EJ140926 listing, but no other information. It is possible that he was Arthur Cole, younger brother (b 1887) of the Charles Cole mentioned below, also of Moor, but evidently survived the war, and so is not listed on any local memorial.

† **Private 242600 Charles Cole** 1/8th Battalion Worcestershire regiment. Soldiers Died records that he was born Pershore, and enlisted at Pershore. Served France and Flanders, killed in action 5th April 1917 age 33. Buried at Templeux-Le-Guerard British Cemetery. Not listed on the Pershore Abbey memorial: he appears to be Charles James Cole, from Hill and Moor. b 1884,

B. Collins Kitchener's Army [EJ140926]

B. Collins Territorials [EJ140926]

B Collins Territorials (EJ140926)

Private Charles Collins Mounted Infantry [AL]

Lance Corpl. 2073 E.G. Collins Worcester Yeomanry - listed as missing in Evesham Journal May 20 1916

Trooper Ernest Collins Worcs. Yeomanry [AL]

Private 20739 Frank Collins 9th Worcesters. Lived at Pershore Fields. Went out 29th Dec 1914. Wounded in the advance on Baghdad. [AV18][AV19][SB]

Private 019255 George Collins A.O.C. Lived in Newlands. [AV18][AV19] See Photo Born in 1883 to George & Lizzie Collins of Head Street. Married in 1910 to Clara Louise Robbins and living in Newlands in

1911. Occupation listed as House Painter. Father of Kathleen, Nora & George Collins. Died in 1950

George John Collins Lived in Newlands [AV18][AV19]

Private Herbert Collins 6th Worcesters [AL]

Gunner 87121 Samuel Richard Collins Royal Garrison Artillery. Lived in Lunn's Yard. [AV18][AV19] Evesham Journal 16 June 1917 - ``Mrs. Collins, of High-street, has heard that her husband, Pte. Sam Collins, has been shot in the left arm. He has two other brothers in the service.''

Corporal Thomas Collins National Reserve (Railway Guard) [AL]

2nd Lieut. William Peter Conly 200 N.T. Squad R.F.C. Lived at Coventry Terrace [AV18][AV19]

Private Edward Thomas Conn 8th Worcesters [EJ140926][AL][SB] Eldest son of Edward and Ellen Conn of 1 Victoria Terrace. Joined up April 1st 1915. Was wounded by January 1917 - see the following entry for his brother Harold.

Thomas Alfred Conn Third son of Edw. Conn. Joined up April 16th 1918, didn't go out. [SB]

Sapper 569987 George Henry Cook Royal Engineers. Lived in Head Street. Sept 1914. (Married Mrs ``Factory'' Twigg's daughter. [AV18][AV19][SB]

William Cook No other information. [SB]

Staff-Sergeant Major James John Cooke. 17th Lancers, 8th Reserve Cavalry Regt. Lived in High Street [AL][AV18][AV19] AV19 says 1st reserve.

Lieut. A.J. Coombe Evesham Journal 29 July 1916 says that this man was wounded, and had been a member of Pershore's hockey club.

Private 13381 Benjamin Coombe 12th Hants. Lived in Head Street. Father of Phyllis. Joined up 1915, went to Salonica Sept. 1915. (AL listed him as a Kitchener's Army recruit) [AL][AV18][AV19][SB]

Private Charles H. Coombe 8th (Res) Worcs. Regt. [EJ141003][AL]

Driver T4/065600 Charles William Coombe Driver in Army Service Corps. Lived in Bachelor's Entry. Grandson of ``Watercress Betsy''. Joined up in 1918 [AV18][AV19][SB]

Private John Coombe King's Royal Rifles. Listed as wounded in 1915 Pershore Almanac. Lived in Newlands [AL][AV18]

Evesham Journal 14 August 1915:-- A BRIEF RESPITE. Pte. Jack Coombe, of the Newlands, Pershore, is home on seven days' leave. He went out with his regiment, the King's Royal Rifles, at the commencement of the war and has taken part in many of the big fights in the western theatre of the war. He was wounded in the wrist in the first engagement of the Aisne, but was out of the French Hospital in time to take part in the battle of Neuve Chapelle. [rest of article is continued under William Hall]

Private Ronald Coombe Inns of Court [AL]

R.E. Coombes Public School Corps

Lieut. Ronald Edmond Coombe *Evesham Journal 22 July 1916 - ``Pershore casualties. Many Pershore officers and men are taking part in the great offensive in France, and each list of casualties published is scanned with grave concern. The past week has been a black one, and the deepest sympathy of the people go out towards those who are sorrowing for the death or disablement of those dear to them. News has been received that Lieut. Cecil H. Lushington is wounded and missing, and Lieut. Ronald Coombe is wounded in hospital. The former was a prominent fruit grower of this district, and the latter was also in the same line of business, being a pupil of Mr. E.P. Whiteley. The Pershore wounded also include Lieut. Robert Lees, son of Mrs Lees, Broad Street, and Corpl. Douglas Hook, son of Sergt. Richard Hook, recruiting officer for Pershore'' Combe, Ronald Edmond. (note surname spelt differently.) Joined the O.T.C. 9/10/14, Regimental Number 1653, served in "E" Company, commissioned in the Royal*

Warwickshire Regiment as 2nd Lieutenant 5/3/15, attached Lancashire Fusiliers, served France and Flanders, attained the rank of Captain, wounded once, awarded the Military Cross. His permanent address in this country is Heathercot, St.Olaves, West Great Yarmouth, Norfolk. Now in India. [AL] lists him as a Private in Inns of Court; [EJ140926] puts him in the Public School Corps (and spells his name ``Coombes''.

Victor George Coombe Brother of Charles William, Joined up 1918. [SB]

Private William Coombe 8th Worcesters. Lived in Melen's Row [AL][AV18]

W. Coombes Kitchener's Army [EJ140926]

W. Coombes Territorials - had served in S. Africa [EJ140926]

Gunner 851134 John William Cooper 2/1 Notts. Bty., R.F.A. Lived in Newlands. [AV18][AV19]

John Henry Cornelius (`Harry') See Photo Farrier Sergeant A Squadron Worcester Yeomanry. Served in Mediterranean (great expeditionary force) disembarked at Alexandria, Egypt 24 April 1915. Lived at Knight's Buildings [AL][EJ140926][AV18]

171763 Thomas George Cornelius A.S.C. Lived in High Street [AV18][AV19] Was he the Sapper T. Cornelius of the Royal Engineers, brother in law of Thomas Pugh, who attended Thomas' funeral March 1917

Private Alfred Joseph Cosnett Knight Buildings. Army Service Corps. Ammunition Corps. Brother of Herbert Thomas. D. South Wales. Went out August 1914 [SB][AL] AL says South Wales Borderers, perhaps confusing with John Henry.

Arthur Cosnett No other information. [SB]

Private Charles Cosnett 8th Worcesters/Reservist [EJ141003][AL]

Trooper 16632 Charles William Cosnett Worcs. Yeomanry. Lived in Knight's Buildings. [AL][AV18][AV19]

Private 30254 George Cosnett 2/4 Dorsets. Lived in Head Street [AV18][AV19]

Private Herbert Cosnett Kitchener's Army [AL]

John Henry Cosnett South Wales Border. Brother of Alfred Joseph. Went out 1914. Lost his leg. Now (1927) in England making artificial limbs. [SB]

Private Joseph Cosnett Brother of Mrs Florence Burt. Head Street. 1/8th Worcesters/reserves. In Italy May 1915 [EJ141003][AL][SB]

Private Joseph Edward Cosnett Army Service Corps. Lived in Knight's Buildings. In England on land. Went out 1915 [AL][AV18][SB]

Private Levi Cosnett 8th Worcesters - had served in S. Africa Lived in Meredith's Row [EJ141003][AL][AV18]

Private 208894 Sydney/Sidney Cosnett 8th Worcesters. Lived in Knight's Buildings. Went out in 1914. [AL][AV18][AV19][SB]

W. Cosnett DISCHARGED. Medically unfit or over age [AL]

Private 16632 Walter Cosnett Lived in Knight's Buildings. Kitchener's Army [AL][EJ140926]; 11th Worcs. [AV18][AV19] Went out in 1914. In Salonica. [SB]

Private William Cosnett National Reserve (Railway Guard) [AL]

William Charles Cosnett Knights Buildings. Worcs. Yeomanry. Served
in England on land. Lost two toes. Went out in 1914. [SB]

F. Cowley Worcesters [EJ151106]

Private 101546 John Charles (``Jack") Cowley 627 Ag. Co. Labour Corps. 7 labour Coy. Living in Head Street, at Mrs. William Mumford's

(Widow of William Mumford) near Mission Hall. October 1916 [AV18][AV19][SB]

Private Leonard Cowley 8th (Res.) Worcs, Regt. [AL][EJ141003]

Private William Cowley Kitchener's Army [AL] In Evesham Journal 28 April 1917, an article entitled `Pershore Officers' quotes some of a letter home by Will Cowley of the Worcesters, about the death of William Price. See that entry for the text.

Gunner 845701 James William Cowper R.F.A. Lived at Coventry Terrace [AV18][AV19]

Charles Crooke Son of Sergt. Samuel Crooke; called up in 1918 aged 18 years.

Sergt. Samuel Crooke National Reserve (Railway Guard) [AL] Stationed in Ireland in 1918: see the entry below for his son William

163438 John Cross R.A.F. Lived in Church Street [AV18][AV19]

G. Curtis DISCHARGED. Medically unfit or over age [AL]

Corporal George Curtis First in R.F.A, then gassed and transferred to Labour Batt. of R.E. Son of Mr Curtis. Went out Christmas 1914 [SB]

Harold A Dancocks 6th Worcesters; was a bandsman around January 1918 (see above). Born 1900, he survived the war: died in 1962, buried at Pershore Cemetery.

Private 2246 Hubert George Daniels 51st Grad. Bn. Devons. Lived in Worcester Street [AV18][AV19]

John Francis Darbyshire Lived in the High Street. [AV18]

Private 236158 Frank Davis Lived in Bridge Street. [AV18][AV19] Listed in Evesham Journal 29 July 1916 as having been a member of Pershore hockey club.

Private J.E.V. Davis 2nd Worcesters [AL]

Col.-Sergt.-Inst. J. Davis   8th Worcesters - had served in S. Africa
[AL][EJ140926]

Rifleman 51269 Percy Edward Davis 15th Royal Irish Rifles. Lived in
Broad Street [AV18][AV19] Listed by Evesham Journal 29 July 1916 as
having been a member of Pershore Hockey Club

Lieut. George Deakin, M.C   Royal Engineers. Lived at the Hall.
[AV18][AV19]

*Evesham Journal 22 September 1917:-- ``2nd Lieut. George Deakin,
R.E., son of Mr. W.R. Deakin, of Pershore, has been awarded the
Military Cross. When in charge of buried cable communications he
displayed the greatest energy and courage in supervising the work of
leading in cables, frequently under heavy shell fire from the enemy's
guns, and in remaining behind after digging parties had been
withdrawn owing to hostile fire, in order to conceal all traces of the
cable from the enemy. His fearless personal reconnaissance's and fine
example of determination to complete his work on all occasions greatly
inspired his men and kept communications open during the
operations."*
*Evesham Journal, 13 April 1918:-- LIEUT. GEORGE DEAKIN, M.C.
WOUNDED. Lieut. George Deakin. the son of Mr. W.H. Deakin, J.P.
and Mrs. Deakin, of The Hall, Pershore, and Bradford Place, Wigan,
received a gunshot wound in the left thigh on Sunday March 24. He is
now lying at the American Red Cross Hospital for Officers at Lancaster
Gate, London, W. The wounded officer received his education at New
College, Harrogate, and Cheltenham Grammar School. He was school
captain at Cheltenham. He was also captain of the football team, and
held the Vassar-Smith Spots Challenge Cup, succeeding his brother,
the late Lieut. Robert Hartley Deakin (Indian Army) attached R.F.C.
who was killed in action on July 22 1917. Five of Mrs Deakin's sons
have entered the Army, all as voluntary soldiers, four having received
commissions into the regular Army. Two graduated from Woolwich,
and two from Sandhurst. The youngest son, Stanley, was
commissioned into the Indian Army in September last at the age of 19,
and is now serving in India.*

Subaltern James Stanley Deakin 84th Punjabis (Indian Army). Lived at The Hall. Commissioned into Indian Army in September 1917, aged 19. [AV18][AV19]

Captain William George Deakin R.F.A. according to Absent Voter list, but see below. Lived at the Hall. [AV18][AV19]
Evesham Journal, 1 June 1918:-- BROTHER OFFICERS DECORATED. Capt. William G. Deakin, Royal Horse Artillery, son of Mr. and Mrs. W.H. Deakin, of The Hall, Pershore, has been awarded the Military Cross for distinguished conduct and devotion to duty in the field. The officer has served in France continuously since he was commissioned in the artillery from the Royal Military Academy, Woolwich, in November 1915. His brother, Lieut. George Deakin, M.C., R.E., who was wounded in the operations of March, has been awarded a bar to the Military Cross. He won the Military Cross in June 1917.

† **Private 15347 Charley Denley** 3rd Battalion Worcester Regiment. Born Pershore; enlisted at Worcester, living at Kidderminster at time of enlistment. Died 18 April 1915 [Soldiers Died]

Corporal Alfred Dennick National Reserve (Railway Guard) [AL]

Private John Dennick Royal Artillery [AL]

Private Thomas Dennick. King's Royal Rifles [AL]

Charles Frankland Dent Lived at Morland House, Bridge Street [AV18]

Private 12833 Evan Joseph Dolphin Kings' Shropshire Light Infantry. Lived in No Gains [AL][Av18][AV19] AL lists him as a Kitchener's Army volunteer.

F. Dolphin Kitchener's Army [EJ140926]

Corporal 28620 Frederick James Dolphin Royal Engineers. Lived in No Gains [AL][AV18][AV19] AL lists him as a Private.

Private Henry Dolphin National Reserve (Railway Guard) [AL]

Private 91889 James Hayward Dolphin 154 Lab. Cps. Lived in Bridge Street. [AV18][AV19]

192886 Lawrence James Dolphin 3rd A.M. Dorsets. Lived in Head Street [AV19]

Lieutenant Arthur Dowty. South Staffordshire regiment [AL]
The 1915 Almanac also mentions that he left Pershore for active service on October 1st 1915, having secured a commission as Second Lieutenant in the 9th Division South Staffordshire Regiment.

Berrow's Worcester Journal 3 October 1915 - PERSHORE OFFICERS DEPARTURE, Mr. H.G. Dowty, fifth son of the late Mr. W. Dowty, chemist, Pershore, who has obtained the position of second lieutenant in the Staffordshire Regiment, left on Monday to join his regiment at Lichfield. He is an old Worcester Grammar School boy. On completion of his schooling, he went in for chemistry. Later he had a desire to join the Army, and eventually entered the Army Medical Corps in December 1911. He remained there until June 1913, when, on the death of his father, he left to come home and assist in the business. He was also at one time an assistant to Mr. C.H. Steward of Worcester.
During the time he has been back in Pershore, he has become very popular, and has closely associated himself with the local Boy Scout movement, acting as instructor for the past nine months. At the outbreak of the war, he .volunteered for any branch in the Army, and signed on into Army Reserve. Congratulations and good wishes will go out to him and his family

Private William Dufty Coldstream Guards [AL]

59667 William Dufty Royal Fusiliers. Lived Little Priest Lane [AV18][AV19]

Sergeant 290954 Joseph Henry Dyer 17th Glosters Lived in ``Dwelling-House" [AV18][AV19]

Private Charles Edginton Kitchener's Army [AL]

W. Edginton Kitchener's Army [EJ140926]

E.J. Edwards Kitchener's Army [EJ140926]

Ernest Edwards Lived in Priest Lane [AV18]

Private Ernest Edwards Royal Artillery [AL]

Lance-Corporal R.C. Edwards Worcs. Yeomanry [EJ140926][AL] EJ140926 lists him as a Trooper. [AL] also includes him as one of those who volunteered for service at the front on August 24th 1914. Pershore heritage centre has a photograph of him in uniform, on horseback; also in a group photo (1915) of Pershore troop No. 3 `D' squadron, and a group photo taken in Egypt. He owned a drapers shop: there is an advertisement in the 1915 Pershore almanac mentioning that the shop is still open. There is a passing mention in Evesham Journal April 7 1917 about Mr. Peter Hanson, who is managing the drapery business at Pershore for Trooper R.C. Edwards, now a prisoner of the Turks.

Evesham Journal 29 December 1917 - IN THE HANDS OF THE TURKS.

From a letter recently received by Mr. Peter Hanson of Pershore, it would appear that Sergt. R.C. Edwards, of the Worcestershire Yeomanry, is in good health, and not very much cast down at his captivity by the Turks. On the very day war was declared against Germany, Sergeant Edwards turned over his business to Mr. Peter Hanson (from whom he purchased it) and joined up. He passed the riding school examination the first day, and after a few month' training was sent out. He was fortunate to emerge unscathed from the Gallipoli campaign, and was afterwards taken prisoner on Easter Sunday, 1916 with other Pershore men, including Sergt. Sid Parkes, Arthur Blizzard, Maurice Sanders etc.; Jack Grundy being killed. In his letter Sergt. Edwards says with relish he learns that another big batch of parcels has arrived at Angora. He goes on: ``I expect you wonder what we do with our time. At present we are working on a railway line right out in the country. We get one day off in seven to mend and do our washing. I have a grand job today, being what we call sive-gar, that is water carrier for the working party. If it were beer or cider I expect I should have a far busier time. Sid Parkes and Arthur Blizzard send their best wishes to the `Mayor' (Mr. Hanson). Parky has become quite an expert with a pick-axe, and Arthur is a marvel on a shovel. We are all in the pink, and being fond of work we make the best of things. The weather here is lovely in the daytime, but the nights begin to get cold. Last year *we had good weather over Christmas, Please remember me to everybody..."*

Guy Leigh Elkington Lived at Amerie Court [AV18]

***Dr Herbert Bree Emerson** Army Service Medical Corps. Lived at Pershore House [AV18] See Photo*

Evesham Journal 28 April 1917 – "DR EMERSON'S ESCAPE". Dr H B Emerson joined the Army Service Medical Corps in the first month of this year, following his junior partner, Dr. A.L. Askham, who after a year's hard work in France has resumed his practice at home. Now that it has been officially reported that the hospital ship, Gloucester Castle, was torpedoed without warning in mid-Channel on the night of March 30-31, we are at liberty to state that Dr. Emerson was performing his duties on that ship, and had a memorable experience. The doctor was one of the many saved by a destroyer, which was within signalling distance, and we are glad to say he is none the worse for his exciting adventure. After a few days at home he has returned to resume his duties." (rest of story continued under the Frank Anstie entry)

Nurse Mary Emerton - *Evesham Journal 2 Nov 1917 ``LOCAL NURSES HONOURED. Miss Mary Emerton, older daughter of Mrs. Emerton, of Pershore has just been awarded the War Office red stripes for service and efficiency as a V.A.D. nurse. She is at present stationed at the Garrison Military Hospital, Harwich, where she has been for the past 18 months."*

Joseph Evans Lived in Newlands [AV18]

Private Thomas Evans Oxford and Bucks Light Infantry [AL]

Alfred John Fagg Lived 2 Church Road [AV18]

A. Farmer Kitchener's Army [EJ140926

66866 Arthur Farr Royal Army Medical Corps. Lived in Nogains. [AV18][AV19]

Corporal Sidney Faulkner Worcs. Yeomanry [AL][EJ140926] Included in a 1915 group photo of the Pershore Troop (no. 3 `D' company); photo in Pershore Heritage centre.

Private 4627 William Fearnside H.A.C. Lived Bridge Street. [AV19]

Evesham Journal, November 6 1915:-- MR W. FEARNSIDE ENLISTS. Mr. W. Fearnside, of Pershore, secretary of the Cooperative Fruit Market and Fruit Growers Association, has resigned these positions and left his business to enlist in the Honourable Artillery Company (Infantry Section) London. His manager, Mr. J. Cliff is left in sole charge of the business, and he will also take over the duties as secretary of the local branch of the Fruit and Vegetable Growers Products Committee, which Mr. Fearnside has carried out with remarkable success. Mr. Fearnside was a member of the Pershore Volunteer Training Corps, and attained creditable efficiency in a course of signalling training under Mr. E.C. Cholmondeley at Eckington.

Private Sidney G. Fell Royal Warwicks [AL]

Private Alfred Ferris 8th Worcesters. Lived at London Bank [EJ141024][AL][AV18]

Arthur Nillson Field R.N.V.R. Lived at Southern House [AV18][AV19]

Private R.G. *Field Evesham Journal, 4 May 1918:-- FORMER PERSHORE MAN WOUNDED. Pte. R.G. Field, late of the Oxford and Bucks Light Infantry, now of Sherwood Foresters, youngest son of Mr. and Mrs. Field, of 21, Water Orton Road, Sunnyside, Oxford, late of Pershore, was wounded on April 17, for the second time, and is now in the 2nd Australian General Hospital, France.*

Evesham Journal October 26 1918:-- PERSHORE MAN GASSED. Pte. R.G. Field, of the Oxford and Bucks. Light Infantry, attached to the King's Shropshire Light Infantry, was gassed on October 4, and is now in 2nd Stationary Hospital, France, but is now going on well. He was wounded twice previously - in July and April this year. He is the youngest son of Mr. and Mrs. C. Field, 21 Wate Eaton-road, Sunnymeade, Oxford, late of Pershore.

† **Private 20365 Robert Footman** 12th Battalion Worcestershire regiment. Actually born in Dudley, Worcs, but included here because he was living in and enlisted at Pershore. Died in the UK 9th June 1915 [Soldiers Died]

108748 Edward Ford Sec 21, R.E. Lived in High Street [AV18][AV19]

Private W. Ford

Private 240482 Frederick John Giles Gloucester Territorials/Gloucesters. Lived in Head Street. Was Serving in Italy in 1918 (see Albert Mark Giles entry above) [AL][AV18][AV19]

Private H325515 Herbert James Giles Worcs. Yeomanry. Lived in Church Row [AV18][AV19]

† **Private 20476 Cyril Benton Glover** 2/8th Battalion Worcs. Regt. Born Pershore, grandson of Ann Glover, of Seaford Grange Cottage, Pershore. enlisted Pershore. Served France and Flanders, died 12th February 1917, aged 19. Buried in Abbeville Communal Cemetery Extension, Somme, France. [Soldiers Died] Not listed on the Abbey Memorial.

17865 Arthur Jervis Goddard Enlisted as Private in Public School Corps, by 1919 was in the R.A.F. Lived at The Bank. [AL][EJ140926][AI][AV18][AV19]

Berrow's Journal, 30 Jan. 1915 has an article ``COMMISSIONS FOR PUBLIC SCHOOL BOYS'', that mentions Arthur Jervis Goddard is the son of Mr. A.C. Goddard, manager of the Capital and Counties' bank, Pershore. He was appointed temporary 2nd lieutenant of Infantry, regular Forces. The last 4 months training had been at Ashtead (Surrey) with the Worcester contingent of the Universities and Public School Old Boys' Force, being the 21st (Service) Battalion Royal Fusiliers.

Lieutenant Frederick Charles Goddard 114 Mahrattas. Lived at The Bank [AV18][AV19]

† **Private 17427 James Godfrey** 4th Battalion Worcestershire Regiment. Born Pershore, enlisted at Worcester (living at Pershore)

Served France & Flanders, killed in Action 23 April 1917. [Soldiers Died].
Not listed on Pershore Abbey War memorial. Listed on Arras War memorial, Pas de Calais, France, (i.e. no known grave): CWGC has no family information listed.

Pte. Bertie Gough

Evesham Journal 11 Sep. 1915. PERSHORE MAN MISSING. The following is taken from a London Newspaper:-- ``No news has been received of Pte. Bertie Gough of 52, Mill-road, Carsholten, who took part in the heavy fighting between the 20th and 30th of July, and unfortunately the worst is feared, as he is known to have been wounded.' ' Much sympathy is felt for his parents who are very highly respected and well known to many at Carsholten and at Pershore, Mr Gough being a native of the latter town. Pte. Gough was 22 years of age and was a smart young fellow and very popular. Joining the 9th Battalion King's Royal Rifles of September 1, he went out to Flanders on May 22. Since then he has been about continually in the fighting line, and on June 16 was gassed at Ypres. This affected his eyes badly and did not keep him out of the trenches. He went into hospital later, but that was due to some complaint caught when his company occupied some German trenches. As soon as he came out he was back in the line and was present at the fighting at Hooge when the Germans used not only poison gas, but their diabolical flame squirts. Mr. and Mrs. Gough have another son, Frank, at the front. He is a lance-corporal in the 6th Gunners. No less than six of their nephews are also serving with the colours." Pte. B.F. Gough, who it is now feared has lost his life, is a nephew of the Misses Gough, Old Manor House, Pershore.

L-cpl. 140328 John Gould   R.E. Lived at 11 Broad Street. [AV18][AV19]

Private 130696 Walter James Gould M.G.C. Lived in Head Street [AV18][AV19]

A. Gray Public School Corps [EJ140926]

Lieutenant Audley Grey. Oxfordshire Light Infantry [AL]

Private Wilfred Gray Public Schools Corps [AL][EJ140926]

Sapper 148178 Arthur Frederick Greenhous Royal Engineers. Lived in High Street. In Wireless section, was in France in 1918. See following entry, [AV18][AV19]

Charles Henry Greenhous Lived in High Street [AV18]

Evesham Journal 27 April 1918 - PERSHORE MAN A PRISONER. About the middle of last month, Mrs. P. Greenhous, of High-street Pershore received news that her youngest son, Charlie, of the Wilts. Regt. was missing. The information came from the chaplain to the regiment, and naturally the uncertainty of their boy's fate has caused the parents a good deal of anxiety. This however, has been partly removed by the receipt of a postcard from him on Wednesday morning, stating that during the recent fighting, when the British were on the defensive, he had been wounded in the left arm and was made a prisoner and taken to Germany. Mr. Greenhous's eldest son Arthur is an engineer in the Wireless section, and is now serving in France. No message has been received from him for several weeks.

Pte Grinnell The following extract is the conclusion of the item for Private F. Soley: there is, as yet, insufficient information as to which member of the family it refers to: Evesham Journal, 2 January 1915, TWO PERSHORE MEN IN 1ST WORCESTERS (contd):- Pte. Grinnell, also of the Worcesters, a reserve, who was called up at the outbreak of the war, is invalided home suffering from frostbite, but he is getting well again, and hoped to be back at headquarters in a few days.

Acting Sergeant 240736 Albert Grinnell See Photos 8th (Res.) Worcestershire Regiment. Born 20th Aug 1897 - son of Charles Grinnell, Head Street [EJ141003][AL][AV18][AV19] Brother of George Enlisted on 29th September 1914. William Grinnell on Roll of Honour. Evesham Journal 15 September 1917 says he was lying wounded in hospital at that time. Married Emily Pratt (Ninny) in 1919 and lived in Little Priest Lane. He was a founder member of Pershore Royal British Legion and Treasurer for many years. He served in the ARP during WW2 and was Divisional

Superintendent of Pershore Division of St John's Ambulance. He worked at RRE Defford during WW2 and was Bell Captain for Pershore Abbey. Died 23rd Nov 1982.

Arthur Grinnell No other information. [SB]

Charles Grinnell Worcesters, training in England in March 1917; see G. Grinnell entry.

Charles Grinnell Worcesters - father of Charles, George, and `Jack' and James - joined Worcesters but was discharged on account of his age. See G. Grinnall entry.

Sergeant Charles James Grinnell Service No 241845 formerly 2016 1/8th Worcesters. Son of Charles Grinnell, Head Street. Brother of George William Grinnell. Lived at 6 Bearcroft Cottage [AV18][AV19] *EVESHAM JOURNAL 17TH NOVEMBER 1926 - THE TOLL OF THE WAR : The funeral of Charles Grinnell (42) of Bearcroft Cottages, Defford Road whose death was briefly announced in the "Journal" last week took place at the cemetery on Thursday afternoon, the Reverend H G Clinch conducting the service. The beautiful collection of floral tributes that covered the coffin indicated the high regard of his friends and neighbours. He was the eldest of the four sons of Charles Grinnell of Head Street who all fought in the Great War. He and his next eldest Brother, William who was wounded at Guillemont Farm fight and killed outright in a later engagement in 1917 belonged to the 1/8th Battalion of the Worcestershire Regiment. Charles was, when mobilised, then a Sergeant and with than rank was demobilised in 1917 after a long time in a South Wales Hospital with five machine gun bullet wounds. The two younger brothers, George and Albert also joined the colours early on and the latter, who was scarce 18 when he went out, rose to the rank of sergeant in the 2/8th Worcesters and was decorated for bravery in the field. The Brothers Grinnell, like thousands of British Tommies who fought and suffered, were ever most uncommunicative about the incidents in which they were personally concerned. Charles, who was a man of powerful physique in 1914 came back but the conflict of BFE was by no means over. Never was a braver fight but put up under the altered conditions of a shattered constitution to provide a living for wife and children in that most exacting profession, market gardening. And, as observant eyes sadly noted, the fight was too much; His last job was that of a* *bricklayer's labourer where at least the weekly wage was certain but he grew steadily weaker and after over three months in the cottage hospital with alternating hopes of recovery, he passed away in that institution leaving a wife and seven children, the eldest of boy of sixteen and the youngest an infant of one. There was a large crowd at the funeral. The Rev H Clifford, Cadet-Major attended and used his car to convey the wife and the children. All the mourners carried a wreath. Mrs Grinnell, Ernest, George, Charles and Albert (sons). Mr and Mrs Charles Grinnell (Father and Mother) Mrs W Garrett (Stroud) Mrs E Goddard, Mrs Sidney Cosnett and Miss Beatrice Grinnell (Sisters) Messrs George and Albert Grinnell (brothers) Messrs E Goddard, J Pratt and S Cosnett (brothers in law) Mrs G Grinnell, Mrs A Grinnell (Sisters-in-law) Mrs Lock (Wyre Mill, Aunt) Mr Frank Lock (cousin) Messrs J Workman, Tom Robbins, S Townsend. Many friends witnessed the last rites at the graveside. The bearers were Messrs Ralph Clarke, J Pratt, S Cosnett and H Howes.*

Sergt. Charles Leach Grinnell 8th Worcesters [EJ140926][AL] EJ140926 says he was in Territorials. Evesham Journal 15 September 1917 says he was now in England.

This is probably a reference to him: (contd. from F. Soley entry) Evesham Journal, 2 January 1915:-- Pte. Grinnell, also of the Worcesters, a reserve, who was called up at the outbreak of the war, is invalided home suffering from frostbite and a shrapnel wound on the hand, but he is getting well again and hope to be back at headquarters in a few days.

Sergt. G. Grinnell D.C.M. Service No 8323 5th Battalion Worcester Regiment Born in Pershore. Age 19 years 4 months on enlistment on 19/11/1908 at Birmingham. He enlisted in the Worcestershire Regiment (Special Reserve) for six years' service and allotted regimental number 8323. He will have served one year with the colours and then spent 5 years on the reserve list.

He had brown hair and eyes and was 5 foot 2.5 inches in height. His next of kin was given as his aunt, Sarah Hamphlett at 173 Darwin Street, Birmingham. He was married and the couple had two children while he was in the army – Alfred James born Pershore 28/1/1912 and Celia Lily born in Birmingham 24/11/1914.

Information kindly supplied by Paul Roberts .

He joined the 5th (Militia) Battalion, the Worcestershire Regiment on 21/11/1908 and completed his training. He was appointed L/Cpl on 9/6/1911 and promoted Corporal on 15/6/1912 and Sergeant in 13/7/1914. He was mobilized on the outbreak of war on 5/8/1914 and was posted to the 3rd Battalion. However he did not land in France until 18/12/1914 and shortly after on Christmas Eve 1914 he was posted to the 2nd Battalion. He was wounded at Richebourg on 16/5/1915 (shell wound to back) and was then sent back to England on 20/5/1915. He was discharged on the termination of his engagement on 18/11/1915 (i.e. the six years that he signed up for in 1908).

He must have re-joined the army later as he is shown as a 2/Lieutenant in the 126th Company, Chinese Labour Corps. He is entitled to the 1914/15 Star Trio named to him as Sergeant. His medals were sent to him at 5 Alexandra Terrace, Westley Street, Birmingham in 1921

Evesham Journal, 31 March 1917:- PERSHORE SOLDIER'S DISTINCTION. [some preamble omitted] Sergt. G. Grinnell of the Worcesters, who previously resided at Broad-Street, Pershore, and is a son of Mr. Charles Grinnell, now living at Birmingham, has been awarded the Distinguished Conduct Medal for bravery and devotion to duty during a raid upon the German trenches near Clery on the night of February 27-28. 1917. Sergt. Grinnell had three brothers, all in the Worcestershire regiment. The eldest, Jack, was killed in action on June 16 1915. A younger brother, Jim, is now serving in Egypt, while the third, Charlie, is training in England.

His father also joined the Worcesters, but was discharged on account of his age"

Evesham Journal, 11 May 1918:- PERSHORE MAN'S DECORATION. Sergt. George Grinnell, a Pershore man, whose home is now in Birmingham, visited the town recently while on furlough, and received the congratulation of many friends on his progress in the army. He won the D.C.M. for gallantry in action on the Somme in 1916, and is now at a cadet school at Bath working on for a commission. An older brother, Jack Grinnell, of the Worcesters, who lived at Pensham, where he was overseer of Mr Blyth's plantation, was killed nearly three years ago, and another brother is with the colours.

Private George Grinnell Territorials [EJ140926][AL] EJ140926 says he was in Territorials

George Grinnell (See Photo) Lived in Head Street [AV18] Known as "Baggy".

Private George Grinnall, 5th Worcesters [AL]

Private James Grinnall 2nd Worcesters [AL] Serving in Egypt in March 1917 - see his elder brother G. Grinnell's entry.

Private John Grinnall 6th Worcesters [AL]

Thomas Guest Pershore's postmaster - Evesham Journal 23 Oct 1915 reported that he had signed up and joined the Royal Engineers. Lived at Post Office House [AV18][AV19]**E. Hall** 3rd Worcesters [AL]

F. Hall Territorials [EJ140926]

Sydney John Hall See Photo *Evesham Journal, 18 May 1918:- PERSHORE MAN A PRISONER. Mr. Thomas Hall, of Sparkhill, Birmingham, and for many years a prominent resident of Pershore, has received information that his son, Sydney John Hall, is a prisoner of war in Germany. He was manager for Messrs. Hall, Lark and Perry, drapers, of Blackpool,Lancs. before joining the Army*

Walter Thomas Hall Lived in High Street [AV18]

Private Walter Hall 8th Worcesters [AL]

Private William Hall 3rd Worcesters -- Listed as wounded in 1915 Pershore Almanac [AL]

Evesham Journal 14 August 1915 [contd. from John Coombe entry]:-- A BRIEF RESPITE. Another Pershore soldier, Pte. William Hall, who went out at the same time [the start of the war], has just obtained his discharge as unfit for further service. He was wounded in four places at

the *battle of Ypres and carries about with him the piece of shrapnel which so mutilated his right arm.*

† Trooper/Lance Corporal Fred Mead Hancock 2nd. (or 1st) Q.O. Worcestershire Hussars (Worcester Yeomanry) died of illness June 25 1915. CWGC register says he's buried in Broughton (St. Mary) Churchyard, Flintshire, United Kingdom: however, a correspondent has told me that he couldn't find the gravestone there, and the newspaper report below gives a different location. He was listed amongst the dead for the previous year in the January 1916 list in the Evesham Journal.

Evesham Journal, 3 July 1915 - PERSHORE YEOMAN'S DEATH. Trpr. Fred Mead Hancock, of the Worcestershire Yeomanry, died from meningitis at Cirencester rather suddenly one June 25. He was taken with sunstroke some weeks ago when drilling with the regiment, and gradually got worse. Before joining the Yeomanry last September deceased was foreman of the goods department at Pershore Station. He had been in the employ of the Great Western Railway Company since the age of fourteen, and had been stationed at Pershore for about three years. He was a son of Mr. C. Hancock, of North Newington, near Banbury, and here he was buried. He was 28 years of age and was engaged to Miss G. Derrett, of Wyre, for whom much sympathy is evinced. The news of Mr. Hancock's death was received with profound regret by his former colleagues at Pershore Station, and by numerous other friends in the district, who held him in high esteem.

Evesham Journal, 10 July 1915 - ``AN ERROR. we made a mistake last week in referring to Lance-Corporal F.M. Hancock of the Worcestershire Yeomanry, who died of meningitis at Cirencester. He was not the foreman porter but the chief clerk of the goods department at Pershore Great Western Station"

Frank R. Harbord Royal Artillery [AB]

189995 Frank William Harris(s) R.A.F. Lived at violet Villa [AV18][AV19] AV19 spells his name with one 's'.

189188 Albert William Hartland R.A.F. Lived in No Gains [AV18][AV19]

R.C. Hartwell Kitchener's Army [EJ140926]

Private 46916 Rawson Hartwell Worcesters. Lived in Priest Lane. [AV18][AV19]

Private William Hawker 8th Worcesters [AL][EJ140926]

Rev. Hawkes-Field Army chaplain, according to Evesham Journal 29 July 1916, which says he'd been a member of Pershore's hockey club.
G. Haynes Kitchener's Army - probably the G. Haynes listed above. Need to check parish registers etc. to be certain [EJ140926]

Frederick Heacock Lived in Priest Lane [AV18][AV19]

86775 Norman Thomas Healey R.F.A. Lived in High Street [AV18][AV19]

Private Albert Heeks Kitchener's Army [AL]

Private 240138 Frank Heeks 1/8th Worcesters [AL] [AV18][AV19] See Photo *Evesham Journal April 1 1916:* ``*Pte. Frank Heeks, of Pershore, attached to the Worcestershire Regiment, was, a chum of his writes, wounded in action on March 14. The letter further states he was shot by a German sniper. Pte. Heeks was home on a short furlough recently. He is a son of Mr and Mrs N. Heeks of the Newlands, Pershore"* NB: *Frank's family inform us that he was gassed and not shot as reported.*

44955 Oliver Heeks 8th Berks. Lived in Newlands. [AV18][AV19]

Trooper George Frederick Hemming Worcs. Yeomanry. Lived in Newlands [AL][AV18]

Private/Trooper James Hemming 8th Worcesters [AL] Yeomanry [EJ140926] Pershore heritage centre has a 1915 group photo of the Yeomanry's Pershore troop (no. 3 `D' company) that includes `Jack Hemming'

L-Cpl. 240015 William James Hemming 8th Worcesters. Lived in Newlands [AV18][AV19]
Private 240015 Alfred John Henderson R.E. (Signals) Lived in High Street [AV18][AV19]

Private James Hewlett 8th Worcesters. Lived in Allesborough cottages [AL][AV18

S. Hewlett DISCHARGED. Medically unfit or over age [AL]

Thomas Hewlett Royal Navy [AL]

William Hewlett Royal Navy. Lived in Church Street [AL][AV18]

F. Hicks Territorials [EJ140926]

A. Higgins 8th (Home Service) Batt. Worcs. Regt. [EJ141024]

† **Private 260517 George Henry Higgins,** 12th Bn. Gloucestershire Regiment. Only son of Sarah Ann and George Higgins, killed in France Nov 17 1917 age 23. Memorial on Sarah and George's grave, Pershore cemetery. CWGC says 7 November - need to check grave. Not listed on Abbey Memorial? Listed on Tyne Cot memorial

Albert `sailor' Hirons Lived at 96 Newlands; Worcester Regiment Army no. 1894; Wounded in the war but survived, came home and married Florence Turvey. Bert was also in the Pershore fire brigade. [AL] lists him in Kitchener's Army.

Joseph Hitchcocks Royal Navy [AL]

Private Edward Hodgkins National Reserve (Railway Guard) [AL]

Cpt 203458 Edward Hodgkins London Rifle Brigade. Lived in Head Street [AV18][AV19]

Trooper Tom Holder Hussars. *Evesham Journal May 4 1918 - WOUNDED THREE TIMES. Mr. John Holder, of Holloway, Pershore, has received bad news concerning his only son, Trooper Tom Holder of the Hussars. He was in action in France the day before Good Friday, and received three wounds, one of which necessitated the amputation* *of the right arm. He is now in a hospital at Bristol. Trooper Holder had been in France for nearly two years, and had seen a good deal of heavy fighting. He was home on leave last December*

Lance-Corporal Hubert Hook Worcester Regiment [EJ141024][AL] AL says he was in 3rd Worcesters, EJ140124 says 6th Batt. Worcs. Regt. Eldest son of Sergt.-Major Hook of Pershore. Evesham journal item about the death of his brother Douglas mentions that Hubert was still serving in the trenches as of February 1917.

Sergeant Richard Lewis Hook Worcs. Yeomanry See Photo [AL][EJ140926] Son of Sergt.-Major Richard Hook of Pershore. Had been a member of Pershore Hockey club, according to Evesham Journal 29 July 1916; Evesham Journal item about the death of his brother Douglas mentions that he ``went through the Gallipoli campaign as a sergeant in the Worcestershire Yeomanry, is now at home"

Lewis Hook

Evesham Journal, 10 February 1917, reporting on Pershore Rural tribunal ---``Richard Lewis Hook (29), single, a time-expired sergeant in the Worcestershire Yeomanry, who went through the Gallipoli campaign, made his second application for conditional exemption. He had been granted a certificate till January. Applicant said he was the son of Richard Hook, Recruiting Sergeant for Pershore District, whose military duties did not allow him to look after his business as a coachbuilder. The application was supported by Mr. Hook, who said his son was in sole charge of the business and was doing a considerable amount of work for agriculturalists. Louis Hook told the Tribunal he was employed four evenings of the week giving musketry instructions to members of the V.T.C. at Pershore, Elmley, and Cropthorne --- Conditional exemption"

Sergt. R. Hook DISCHARGED. Medically unfit or over age [AL] This is most likely Sergt.-Major Richard Hook, who was the Recruiting Sergeant for Pershore district by 1917, and three of whose sons are listed above.

Bdr. 26456 George Henry Hooper R.G.A. Lived Pershore Fields [AV18][AV19]

Lance-Corporal 18291 Gabriel Hopkins 11th Somerset Light Infantry. Lived in Bridge Street. [AV18][AV19] Evesham Journal October 5 1918: SHOT BY A SNIPER. Pte. Gabriel Hopkins, son of Mrs. J. Hopkins, of Bridge-street Pershore, was shot through the thigh by a sniper, and is now in hospital at Clapton-on-Sea. Everybody hopes he will have a speedy recovery. Pte. Hopkins is a good sportsman. He played International Hockey, and was a valued member of the local team. He is also a fine footballer and cricketer.
William Horton Town Guard [AL]

Private 265100 Walter Howard Howell 7th Somersets. Lived in Bridge Street. [AV18][AV19]

Private M2/176724 John Edwin Howes A.S.C. Lived at 3 Priest Lane [AV18][AV19]

Private Harold John Howes Service No: 161738 Machine Gun Corps lived at Knights Buildings - son of John Joseph Howes. Believed to have served abroad in latter part of the war. Was Chief Auctioneer at the Co-op in Defford Road later in life. Married an Eckington girl - Mabel Halling whose brother Gilbert was killed in Palestine.

John Joseph Howse Lived at Knight's Buildings [AV18] Enlisted 7th December 1914. Royal Engineers. Carpenter by trade. Lived at Knight's Buildings [AV18] Joined the Army on 7th December 1914. Transferred to the RFC 11th December 1917 and the RAF on 1st April 1918. Employed at Norton Barracks as a carpenter and discharged on 24th December 1918 with chronic rheumatism and injury to hand pending surgery.

Private Martin Howse 6th Worcesters. *Evesham Journal 29 July 1916 - ``Mrs. J. Howse of Knight's-terrace, Pershore, has been informed that her son, Pte. Martin Howse of the Worcesters, is wounded and in hospital. He is but a lad, 19 next week, and has been wounded twice, the first time at the Dardanelles, and now in the recent offensive move in France. His father is in the Royal Engineers" [AL] Ref AL spells his name ``Howse"*

Evesham Journal, 21 September 1918:-- NEWS AT LAST. In reply to persistent enquiries, Mrs. J. Howes, of Knight's Buildings, Pershore, *(whose husband is in the army), learnt from a letter sent last August by the officer commanding the 77th Field Ambulance in France, that her son, Pte. Martin Howes, of the 3rd Worcesters, was admitted to a main dressing station on the 27th of May, suffering from gunshot wounds in the left knee and foot. At the time there were very severe military operations in progress, and owing to the situation becoming acute, this dressing station had to be hurriedly abandoned. It was only possible to evacuate to the casualty clearing station a small percentage of the cases there before it fell into the hands of the enemy. ``If, therefore", the letter stated, ``his name has not been reported as passing through a medical unit on the lines of communication, it is feared he is one of those captured by the enemy." All doubt has now passed, as Mrs. Howes has received a postcard, bearing the formidable name of a German town, that her son is in captivity, and the German censor graciously permits the prisoner to add the ubiquitous English word, ``Cheerio". Pte. Martin Howes, known among his Pershore friends as Sonny Howes, has been wounded four time, the first occasion being when he was out with the Mediterranean Force. He was then only 18 years old. He has had hard and exciting experiences during his service.*

R. Howes   Kitchener's Army [EJ140926]

Lt.-Com. Charles Edward Hudson   R.N.R. Lived in Abbey Place [AV18][AV19]

Major William Warren Hudson   11th Worcesters. Son of Lieut. Col. and
Mrs. A.H. Hudson of Wick House. Serving in Salonika in October 1916. Listed on the Wick Roll of Honour where he is listed as a Lt. Col.

Private Edward Hughes   6th Worcesters [AL]

W. Hughes   Reservist [EJ140926]

Lieut. Christopher Munro Humphries   3rd S. Highlanders. Lived in Bridge Street [AV18][AV19]

Ernest William Hunt   Lived in No Gains [AV18]

Major Walter John Hunt Lived in Worcester Street. refs. [AL][EJ140926][AV18][AV19] [AL] lists him as Captain in 8th Worcesters (Territorials); several years later, [AV19] has him as a Major att. 36th Northumberland Fus.

Thomas Albert Hutton Listed by [AL] as a private in the Public Schools Infantry. By [AV19], four years later, he's listed as a captain. (see below). Lived in High Street. Also listed in [AV18], [EJ140926]

Evesham Journal July 3 1915:-- LIEUT. BERT HUTTON. It may not be generally known in the locality that Mr. Bert Hutton, of Pershore, who in September last attached himself to the Public Schools Battalion of the Royal Fusiliers, has now received a commission as 2nd Lieut. in the 5th Worcesters. Lieut. Hutton had a short furlough last weekend, and told his friends he expected shortly to be sent out to the front.

Evesham Journal 20 May 1916:-- LIEUT. B. HUTTON IN HOSPITAL. Mrs. Hutton of High Street, Pershore, has received a telegram from the War Office this week telling her that her husband, Lieut. Bert Hutton, has been sent to a hospital at Karachi, India, suffering from dysentery. Lieut. Hutton was with the relief force under General Gorringe, in Mesopotamia, and it was here he contracted the illness
EJ 29th July 1916 mentions that Bert Hutton had been a member of Pershore's Hockey club.

Evesham Journal, 14 October 1916:-- ``COMMISSION FOR PERSHORE MAN. Mr Bert Hutton, the well-known operatic singer, of Pershore. who is now in hospital in Bomabar, has been promoted 2nd Lieut. and is attached to the Worcesters. He went through the Gallipoli campaign"

Evesham Journal, 21 October 1916:-- ``PERSHORE OFFICERS. Our reference to Lieut Bert Hutton, formerly of Pershore, was incorrect. He has recently been promoted to 1st Lieutenant, having obtained his commission from the Public School Corps in May 1915, he has seen a lot of fighting in Gallipoli, and in connection with the relief force in Mesopotamia. He is at present in in Hospital in Bombay."
(remainder of story continued under Frank J. Nicholas)

Evesham Journal, 28 April 1917:-- ``CAPT. B. HUTTON SERIOUSLY WOUNDED. Mrs. Hutton, of High-street, Pershore, has received official information that her husband, Capt. Bert Hutton, of the Worcesters, was seriously wounded in the recent fighting in Mesopotamia. This is the first intimation that Mrs. Hutton received that her husband had been promoted to the rank of Captain. Capt. Hutton joined the service in the early months of the war, and has seen much fighting with the Turks." Evesham Journal 26 May 1917:-- ``PERSHORE AT THE FRONT" A short time ago Mrs. Hutton, of High Street Pershore, received official information that her husband Capt. A. Hutton, had been seriously wounded in Mesopotamia, and was in hospital at Baghdad. She called for further particulars, and last week received a further communication from the War Office that Capt. Hutton was progressing favourably. Many Pershore people will share in the relief which this later message gives." (remainder continued under Robert Lees)

Evesham Journal 23 March 1918 - ``CAPT. BERT HUTTON MENTIONED. Capt. A.B. Hutton was mentioned in the despatches by Sir Stanley Mande, published last week, for gallant and distinguished service in Mesopotamia, and Pershore people generally are proud of the honour he has won for himself. Before the war Capt. Hutton was foreman over one of the departments at the Atlas Works. He is a fine bass singer, and his ability in amateur opera was recognised and appreciated in Pershore, Evesham, Worcester and Droitwich, at each of which places he at various times assisted the local societies. Capt. Hutton joined the University O.T.C. in September 1914, obtained his commission in May 1915, and went to Gallipoli September 1915, and was in both evacuations - Suval Bay and Hellas Point. He went to Mesopotamia and was in the Kut relief fighting, and also the Tigris Campaign. He assisted in the capture of Baghdad, and was seriously wounded 50 miles beyond that city. He is now on important military work at Belgaum, India."

A.T. Hyde 15342 Worcestershire Regiment. Listed among the wounded Evesham Journal 20 May 1916

20727 Arthur James Ireland 4th Worcesters. Lived at 3, Knight's Buildings. [AV18][AV19] Appears to have been listed twice in AV19 for some reason (nos. 4567, 4735

Private Charles Izard 15th Hussars [AL] Evesham Journal 9 June 1917 - ``PERSHORE MAN'S EXCITING EXPERIENCE. In a letter to his wife, Pte. Charles Izard, of Pershore, who is attached to the Royal

Bucks. tells how he is in hospital in Marseilles with fever, and recounts an exciting experience he had on the 4th of May, when the ship he was on was torpedoed and went down. He and others were picked up by a Japanese destroyer, but many were drowned. They were stranded in Italy for a week, and then were sent by train to Marseilles. Pte. Izard had been some years in the army. Prior to the outbreak of war he was groom to General Hunter at Farnham."

Frederick Izard Lived in High Street [AV18]

Private Percy Izard Kitchener's Army [AL][EJ140926]

Pte. Henry `Ensor' Jones   Town Guard [AL] Evesham Journal 27 March 1915, Continued from Sergeant Henry Jones entry: ``His father, Pte. Henry Jones, known everywhere in the Pershore district as `Ensor' Jones, is at present doing duty guarding railway bridges. He went through the South African Campaign, and belonged to the National Reserve. He can play, and play cleverly, almost every musical instrument there is, and his entertaining proclivities are so appreciated where he is billeted that the officers have recently presented him with an English concertina, Pte. Jones was groundsman for Pershore Hockey Club."

Private Henry Jones Royal Warwicks [AL]

Sergeant Henry Jones 1st Worcesters. *Evesham Journal, 27 March 1915:--* ``*PERSHORE SERGEANT WOUNDED. Sergt. Henry Jones, of the 1st. Worcesters, who has been wrongly reported as killed in some papers, is lying badly wounded in Hampstead-road Temperance Hospital, London, but is progressing favourably towards recovery. He was invalided home from the front last week with three bullet wounds in the right arm. While taking part in an engagement two months ago he was shot in the hand, but the wound was not sufficiently serious to necessitate his coming home. Sergt. Jones joined the Army before he was out of his teens, and was quickly promoted to the rank of sergeant." (rest of article refers to his father, `Ensor' Jones, and is listed under his heading)*

Sergeant Jack Jones Evesham Journal, 31 July 1915, in a report on the death of Arthur Biddulph (see above) mentions that Mrs Jones' brother, Sergt. Jack Jones, ``was badly wounded in the fight at Neuve

Chapelle - he is a Worcester man and has five brothers now serving in the trenches, and two on garrison duty" - since Mrs Biddulph was the daughter of 'Ensor' Jones, these brothers must fit the Pershore men category....

Private John Jones 1st Worcesters [AL]

Gunner Norman Jones Royal Field Artillery [AL]

A. Keen Lance-Sergt. Yeomanry [EJ140926] A 1915 group photo of the Yeomanry's Pershore troop (no. 3 `D' squadron) has a ``Lt. Cay. Keen" which may be him; photo in the Pershore Heritage centre.

John Freeman Kettell Lived in Priest Lane [AV18]

Private William Keyte Kitchener's Army [AL]

23515 Henry Kings 4th Worcesters. Lived in Ganderton's Row [Av18][AV19]

Private William Kings Grenadier Guards - Evesham Journal 19 Feb 1916 recounts that ``though he was in the first expeditionary force to France, and has taken part in some of the hottest fights, has so far escaped without a scratch" Brother of Arthur W. Kings

Evesham Journal 9 Dec 1916 (contd. from Arthur Kings above) --- ``William, the elder brother of the late Lance-Corpl. Kings, was also in the Grenadier Guards, and after 22 months' hard and continuous service on the French and Belgian fronts has just been discharged as a time-expired man and for medical reasons. He was a reservist and was a member of the Birmingham City Police when war broke out. He has now re-joined the force. William, though also of exceptionally fine physique, was not so tall as his brother. On June 12 1915. the date of the Lance Corporal's 21st birthday, the brothers met for the first time as soldiers at a village called Festerburgh, Northern France."

Cpl. 16887 George Kirby 9th Gloucesters. Lived in High Street [AV18][AV19]

Trooper John Alfred Knight Worcs. Yeomanry. Lived at White Horse Hotel [EJ140926][AL][AV18] Pershore Heritage centre has a

1915 group photo of Pershore Troop (No. 3 `D' company) that includes `Jack Knight'

William James Knight Lived in High Street [AV18]

Frederick William Latham Head Street [AV18]

Private William Latham 8th Worcesters [AL]

William Edward Latham Lived in Head Street [AV18]

Charles James Leach Worcestershire Regt. See photo Lived at Bearcroft [AV18] Died 1928.

Private Alexander (or Alick) Yates Lees 8th Worcesters/Territorials. Lived in Bridge Street [AL][EJ140926][AV18]

Private Andrew Lees 8th Worcesters/Territorial Lived in Bridge Street [EJ140926][AL][AV18]

Andrew Yates Lees died 10th June 1925 ``as a result of war service" aged 25 years. Buried in Pershore cemetery. Likely to be the same person as Private Andrew Lees above.

Lieut. Robert Cowan Lees R.F.A. Son of Mrs. Lees, Bridge Street, in a list of the wounded published in Evesham Journal 22 July 1916 (See Ronald Coombes entry for full article) Had been a member of Pershore's hockey club, according to a mention in the Evesham Journal 29 July 1916 Listed in [AV18][AV19].
Evesham Journal 26 May 1917 - ``PERSHORE AT THE FRONT. (continued from the Albert Hutton item) - Lieut. Robert Lees, of the R.F.A., son of Mrs. Lees of Bridge-street, has been wounded a second time, and is now in hospital at Reading. The gallant deeds of the Pershore men at the same action brings honour to the town to which they are connected. In one month, three officers gained distinction for their bravery" - (see entries for Capt. Watson, Lieut. Meysey Hammond, Sergt. Grinnell)

Francis William Lewis High Street [AV18]

Pte. Wm. Lewis 5th Worcesters. Listed as Prisoner of War in 1915 Pershore Almanac [AL]

† **Sergt.-Major 17161 William H. Lewis** Royal Warwickshire regiment, died on Tuesday, 19th June 1917. Age 31. Buried at Cairo War Memorial Cemetery, Egypt. CWGC database describes him as the husband of Edith Ethel Worton Lewis, of 15, Rectory St., Wordsley, Stourbridge, Worcs. He is apparently not listed on any Pershore area memorial, but see the following extract from *Evesham Journal, 30 June 1917:* ``The Roll of Honour of Pershore Post office, which consists of the names of Corporal H. Wedgebury (missing, believed killed), Corpl. C. Twigg, Pte. H. Dufty, and Pte. Percy Smith, now includes that of Company-Sergt.-Major William Lewis, of the Royal Warwicks. Mrs. Lewis, who resides in Plough-lane, received a letter from the War Office on Tuesday Week, intimating her husband was seriously ill in hospital at Cairo, and the following day came a wire announcing his death. Much sympathy is felt for the widow, who is left with one child. Sergt. Major Lewis before the war was rural postman from Pershore to Peopleton. Formerly he was stationed at Eckington. He was a good type of the non-commissioned officer, being a reservist in the Royal Warwicks, he mobilised on the 4th August 1914, and had the honour of being a unit in Gen. French's ``contemptible little army" which checked the onward rush of the Prussian hosts towards the gates of Paris, and made possible the winning of the war for the Allies. He was in the historic battle of the Marne, where he fought and bled, and after convalescence he again took his place in the fighting line, and went through many more battle. He was subsequently sent to Egypt."*

Francis William Lewis R.A.F. Lived in High Street. [AV19] Appears to be listed twice in AV19, refs. 5362 and 5370

Private Jack Long Kitchener's Army [EJ140926]; 8th Worcesters [AL]

Hubert Long Lived at Cemetery cottages [AV18]

Private 34100 Cyril Henry Ludlow 13th Gren. Guards. Lived in Head Street [AV18][AV19]

Private George Ludlow 8th Worcesters. Lived in Head Street
[EJ141003][AL][AV18]

Captain Lionel Frederick Machin K.O.S.B. Lived in Stanhope
House.
[AV18][AV19] NB. [EJ140926] and [AL] list him as a private in
(Sandhurst) Public School Corps.
Second-Lieut. Norman Frederick Machin D.S.M Coldstream
Guards. Lived in Stanhope House. His name appears twice in ref.
AV19: no. 4743 lists him as a Lieutenant, 4572 lists him as a Captain.
[AV18][AV19]

*Evesham Journal, 25 November 1916 - ``PERSHORE MAN'S
GALLANTRY. Second-Lieut. Norman F. Machin, of the Coldstream
Guards, has been awarded the Distinguished Service Medal for
Gallantry in the field. He led and rallied his men under heavy barrage
fire, until he fell wounded. Prior to joining the colours Lieut. Machin was
a market gardener at Pershore, and was a pupil with Mr. E.P. Whiteley,
hon. secretary of the Pershore Fruit Growers' Association. He is a
nephew of Miss Sainsbury, Stanhope House, where he resided.*

Private J. Mann Kitchener's Army [AL]

Private Joseph Mann 5th Worcesters [AL]

† **2nd. Lieutenant Kenneth Mann** 4th Suffolks. Killed at some time
before January 1916 according to [EJD16. but doesn't appear in n
Soldiers died or the CWGC database.
Private Arthur Manton 8th Worcesters [AL][EJ141003]

Private Joseph Manton Kitchener's Army [AL]
J. Manton Kitchener's Army [EJ140926]
Private Joseph Manton 8th Worcesters [AL]

Private Charles Marshall National Reserve (Railway Guard). [AL]
Discharged from army around June 1918

Private Philip Marshall 8th Worcesters/reservist [AL][EJ140926] Son
of John and Rose Ellen Marshall of top Newland, Pershore. Badly
gassed in action, January 1917, and by June 1917 was then a

substitute working on the land at Evesham (source: Evesham Journal 4 June 1917 - see the James Annis entry)

42919 William Marshall London Regiment. Lived in Newlands. Son of Charles and Ellen Marshall of Lower Newlands. Serving in front line in 1918, according to the death notice for his brother Charles. [AV18][AV19]

† **Gunner 162869 Walter Martin** 146th Siege Bty. Royal Garrison Artillery. Son of David and E.M. Martin of Pershore, husband of Christina E. Martin of 18 Hill Avenue, Worcester. Died 20 December 1917 age 34. Buried St Albans Cemetery, Hertfordshire Ex-pupil of Worcester Grammar school, listed on the school's memorial N.B. Had moved out of Pershore, not listed on Pershore Abbey memorial.

Evesham Journal 19 January 1918 - GUNNER WALTER MARTIN'S DEATH. The death of Gunner Walter Martin, of the Royal Garrison Artillery, brings sorrow to many people in the Pershore district, who knew him well and esteemed him highly. Prior to May last, when he joined the colours, he was a clerk in the Old Bank of Worcester, and his young widow and child live at 18 Hill-avenue Worcester. Mr. Martin was sent to France in less than five months' training, and in a hot engagement in which he was unrelieved with the guns for a considerable time, he caught a chill, and various complications supervened, which terminated his life at St. Alban's Red Cross Hospital. He was the eldest son of Mr. David Martin of Cheltenham, formerly of the firm of Messrs. Fearnside and Martin, printers, of Pershore. A memorial service was held at the Primitive Methodist Chapel at Drakes Broughton, at which place of worship he succeeded his father as organist, his gratuitous services being greatly valued by the members. For some years, he and his wife were members of Pershore Amateur Operatic Society, and Mr. Martin took the title role in a most successful production of the ``Mikado''. For some time, too, he acted as hon. secretary of the society. Deceased was 34 years of age. Another brother is in the Army.

Private S/355531 Franz Alfred Charles Mason A.S.C. Lived at Knotty Elms [AV18][AV19] *Evesham Journal 30 June 1917 - ``PERSHORE AND THE WAR. Mr. Charles Mason (the organist at the Abbey Church) has been called up, and is attached to the Army Service Corps. His successor is Miss Pritchard, of Oxford.... ''*

There are more details in this story about Pershore men, listed under William Lewis.

Evesham Journal January 25 1919:-- PERSHORE ORGANIST IN FRANCE. The Paris ``Daily Mail" records that there was a large gathering of soldiers and sailors at the Seamen's Institute of Rouen, recently, where an excellent Christmas dinner was followed by a good musical programme. Pte. F.A.C. Mason, R.A.S.C. being at the piano. Mr Mason is the well-known organist at Pershore Abbey, to which post he hopes to return as soon as possible. He has been in the Army for about 18 months, and soon after he landed in France he was appointed organist to All Saints Church in Rouen. He is the son of Mrs. Mason and of the late Mr Edward Mason, of St Dunstan's Crescent, Worcester.

Pte. M/3410195 James McCormick jun. M.T.A.S.C. Lived in Bridge Street. [AV18][AV19]

John Victor McCormick Lived in Bridge Street [AV18]

Lieut. McIntosh Evesham Journal 28 April 1917, extract of article titled `Pershore Officers': ``It is officially stated that Lieut. McIntosh has been wounded and is in hospital in Oxford. A year ago last February Lieut McIntosh married Miss Wallis, daughter of Mr. George Wallis, builder, of High-street, Pershore."
Sh.-smith 2444 R. Meadows Worcester Yeomanry - listed as missing in Evesham Journal 20 May 1916

Albert Mence Lived at No Gains [AV18]

Private Edward Middleton 8th Worcesters
[AL]

Frederick John Middleton See Photo
Lived in Newlands [AV18]

Private 60546 William Middleton
S. Staffs. Lived in Knotty Elms [AV18][AV19]

Lance-Corporal Charles Milward Worcs. Yeomanry See photo of him on horseback, dated as 1915, at King's Lynn. Moved to the Infantry, fought in both battles of the Somme where he was gassed. Ended up as a Quarter Master Sargeant.

Charles Thomas Milward Lived in Broad Street [AV18]

Mitchell 3rd Battalion Rifle Brigade.
Berrow's Journal 30th Jan 1915 – PERSHORE MAN'S EXPERIENCE. Mrs. Mitchell of Southern House, Broad Street Pershore, has heard from her son, who went out with the first expeditionary force and is now serving with the 3rd battalion Rifle Brigade. Speaking of the hardships experienced, he says that at the time of writing they were having a nice day after a long spell of bad weather. Since being out at the seat of war he has not had his clothes off or even a chance to get a wash. They cannot even wash anything, as there is no chance to dry them. He is suffering from rheumatism owing to the wet and mud. The men are being supplied with 2oz. of tobacco per week, but they cannot get any cigarettes.

Private Christopher Moore See photo 10th Hussars Lived in Head Street [AL][AV18]

102324 Walter Moore R.F.A. Lived at Drill Hall [AV18][AV19]

James Moulson Wireless section, Royal engineers. Eldest son of Mr. and Mrs. F.W. Moulson. Serving in the army abroad in September 1918; known to be in Belgium in December 1918. (see Arthur Moulson entry above)

Private Charles Mumford Kitchener's Army [AL]

Private 255305 Frederick Mumford 2/6 Sussex. Lived at Head Street. [AV18][AV19]

Private H. Mumford Kitchener's Army [AL]
H. Mumford Brabant's Horse - had served in S. Africa [EJ140926]

Temp.-Lieut. Hugh Mumford Worcester Regiment. Lived at Three Springs [AV18] Pershore Almanac 1915 says he was amongst those who'd volunteered for service at the front on the 24th August 1914. *Evesham Journal 22nd January 1916: ``Temp.-Lieut. Hugh Mumford of the Army Service Corps is transferred to be Temp.-Lieut. of the Second Reserves Worcestershire Regiment, dated January 1st 1916"* *Evesham Journal 29 July 1916 says he'd been a member of Pershore's hockey club.*

Evesham Journal 16 June 1917 - ``Capt. Hugh Mumford, who is now attached to the Worcesters at Salonika, is reported wounded and in hospital."

Private Walter Mumford 8th Worcesters/Reservist [EJ140926][AL]

Private 522130 Walter Mumford 627 Ag. Co. Labour Corps. Lived in Head Street [AV18][AV19] A Private W. Mumford was one of the bearers at the funeral of Harry Smith in early 1918.

Harry Need Royal Engineers. Son of W. Need the Abbey's Verger. See John Need entry following.

Sergeant Thomas Need 8th Worcesters Lived in Priest Lane [AL][AV18] Son of W. Need, the Abbey's verger. See John Need above.

Private 515014 William Charles Neil 1/14 Lond. R. Lived at Lloyds Bank. [AV18][AV19]

Andrew Henry Newell Lived at `Binholme' [AV18]

Private Henry Newell Royal Warwicks [AL]

147714 Harry Newman R.A.F. Lived in Newlands. [AV18][AV19]

Trooper W.L. Newport Worcs. Yeomanry [AL]

Lieut. Frank James Nicholas According to Evesham Journal, 29 July 1916, had been member of Pershore Hockey club: had joined the O.T.C. Lincoln's inn, had recently been gazetted as Lieut. in the 11th

Gloucesters, and has taken a platoon out to France. AV19 says he was in the 3rd Gloucesters. Lived in Bridge Street [AV18][AV19]

Evesham Journal, 21 October 1916 (contd. from Albert Hutton record): ``Mr A.J. Nicholas, youngest son of Mr and Mrs Frank Nicholas, of Bridge-street, Pershore, has been promoted to 1st Lieutenant. He is attached to the Gloucesters, and has been for some weeks in the fighting line. Lieutenant Nicholas is the well-known County hockey player'' [note that the Journal appears to have got one of his initials wrong -everything else is a good match]

Evesham Journal September 29th 1917 - ``LIEUT. FRANK NICHOLAS WOUNDED. Mr. F. Nicholas of Messrs. Nicholas Bros. builders and contractors, Pershore, received a wire from the War Office this week informing him that his son, Lieut. Frank J. Nicholas, Gloucester Regt., was admitted into the stationary hospital at Boulogne seriously ill with gunshot wounds in the right thigh. Better news arrived the following morning from the wounded officer himself, who said the bullet had been extracted, and he was going on very comfortably. Lieut. Nicholas, who before joining the Inn of Court O.T.C. in 1915, was in the Land Valuation Office at Worcester, went to France in June 1916, and has experienced a good deal of warfare. In February this year he was promoted to the rank of Lieutenant. he is well known in the county as a first-class hockey player. He played three successive seasons for Worcestershire, and was a most prolific scorer for his own local team at Pershore, where he played centre forward. Cricket, tennis, or any other game, he always excelled, and was generally regarded as a good, all-round sportsman.''

141567 John James Nicholas 63 Div., M.T. Co. A.S.C. Lived in Bridge Street [AV18][AV19]

H. Nicholas DISCHARGED. Medically unfit or over age [AL]

Harry George Nicholas Lived at Defford Road [AV18]

234709 Walter Henry Nicholas A.S.C. Lived in Bridge Street [AV18][AV19]

Walter Henry Nott Lived in Union House [AV18]

Pioneer 316505 David Joseph Rouse Nutting R.E. Lived in Broad Street [AV18][AV19]

Frank Nutting Lived at Pershore Fields [AV18]
Probably the elder brother of Arthur Douglas Nutting; see above.

Sapper 19098 William James Overd Royal Engineers. Lived in Newlands [EJ141017][AL][AV18][AV19]

E. Page Worcesters (Territorials) [EJ151106]

Corporal 2721 Sid G. Parkes Worcester Yeomanry. Listed as missing in Evesham Journal 20 May 1916; a letter home from R.C. Edwards printed in the 29th December Evesham Journal (see his entry) reveals that Parkes was amongst the men captured by the Turks on Easter Sunday 1916, and was still a prisoner in late 1917. (N.B. the letter lists him as a sergeant) Pershore heritage centre has a 1915 group photo of Pershore Troop (No. 3 `D' company) that includes him, also a group photo in Egypt.

Flt.-Sgt. 10792 Cecil James Partridge No 50 A.T.S. Lived in Mill House. [AV18][AV19]

A.W. Phillips A.V.C. [EJ151106]

Harry Calvin Luther Phillips Lived at Defford Road [AV18]

49792 Henry John Phillips 1st Northamptons 48th of Foot. Lived in New Road [AV18][AV19]

Private 85662 Herbert Phillips 70th Co. M.G.C. Lived in High Street. [AV18][AV19]

2nd-Lieutenant Tom Phillips Royal Engineers
Evesham Journal 28 April 1917, extract of article titled `Pershore Officers': ``Mr. Tom Phillips, youngest son of Mr. George Phillips, of Pershore, has been gazetted 2nd Lieutenant, and attached to the Royal Engineers. He joined the army a month ago and was private in the Royal Artillery.''

Private 243061 John Pugh Plimmer King's Liverpools, 424th Army Ag. Coy. Lived in Broad Street [AV18][AV19]

Private Alfred Porter Royal Army Medical Corps. Listed as Prisoner of War in 1915 Pershore Almanac. Lived in Church Row [AL][AV18]
Evesham Journal 20 March 1915 - *PERSHORE POSTMAN PRISONER. Reservist Alfred Porter, of the Newlands, Pershore, who went to the front in the early stages of the war attached to the Army Medical Corps, has been a prisoner for some months in Sennelgar, Germany. His wife has received several postcards from him, and in a recent one it seems significant that German Censorship should allow him, after stating he is doing very well, to ask for ``anything in the eating line, cheese, butter, bacon, bread, tea, coffee, cocoa, in fact nothing would come amiss." Prior to the war, Pte. Porter was a rural postman attached to Pershore Post Office and went round the Cropthorne district. He is a native of Badsey, near Evesham.*

Evesham Journal 3 July 1915 - *PERSHORE PRISONER'S RETURN. Before the war Pte. Alfred Porter, Church-row, Pershore, was a reserve in the Royal Army Medical Corps, and was employed as a rural postman at Pershore Post Office. He went out to France at the beginning of August, and was taken prisoner with many others at Mons. He wrote to his wife and children frequently, and a month generally intervened between the date of his latter and delivery. He always asked for food, and she sent him regularly every week home-made bread and provisions, which absorbed a good proportion of his allowance. On Wednesday morning she was greatly surprised and elated to receive a wire, stating he was safely landed in England. A letter arrived from him in the afternoon, stating he was then in King George's Hospital, London, but hoped to be home shortly. He intimated he was more than glad to be free of Germany, as he would have starved but for what she sent him. Mrs. Porter is a little perturbed to learn he is in hospital, as he never mentioned any injuries or illness to her. The same day she received the wire and later she also received a letter written by her husband from his internment camp in Germany, but in this he did not mention that he expected to be sent home.*

DON'T MENTION THE WAR. In writing from Germany to his wife, Pte. Porter frequently cautioned her never in replies to mention the war. ``It will be better for me if you don't." he stated. Presumably such cautionary advice was not given by another prisoner of the Germans to his wife who lives at Sale Green, near Upton Snodsbury. The story goes that in a reply to his letters, which always dwelt wistfully on the hope of returning home, she expressed her great desire that when he did come he would bring the Kaiser's head with him. The correspondence ceased abruptly, and the good wife has since felt anxious as to her husband's safety.

Evesham Journal 10 July 1915 - HOME FROM GERMANY. Private Alfred Porter, of the Royal Army Service Corps, who has been ten months a prisoner in Germany, came home to Pershore this week. He returned with the recent batch of exchanged prisoners. The `wire' announcing his arrival in England came from King George's Hospital, London, and his wife was concerned at this, thinking he was wounded, which, however, he had not stated in his many letters to her from Germany. But Private Porter says they only went there to have a bath, some refreshments, and a new rig-out. The Germans were not concerned in returning them clean and tidy; they had relieved them of everything that was of any value, and sent them back with ill-fitting and most atrocious garments. What surprises him most now he has come back is the strength of Kitchener's new army and the appearance of it. He had no idea recruiting was going so strong in England, and after paying a hurried visit to Aldershot says he has never seen finer looking soldiers in his life. He has brought back as a relic a piece of German black bread, and most unappetising looking stuff it is. This bread with boiled swedes and horse beans was what they chiefly lived on out there, and he says he is bound to confess, although he never seemed to have enough to eat, that he never felt better in his life. The aroma of the boiled pork, which the German soldiers used to have served out to them with similar vegetable, so watered the palates of our poor chaps, he said, that it was positively maddening. One day, a British `Tommy' succeeded in purloining a piece, but before he had completely devoured it he was caught and as a punishment was tied to a tree for several hours. Pte. Porter was caught with 130 of his comrades while burying the dead at Mons on the Tuesday following the great retreat. They were stripped of everything that night on Mons station, and were served with wretched clothing. It took thirty-two hours to reach their destination at Sennelager. They were conveyed in cattle trucks, and en route were much jeered at and insulted by the German populace of the towns and villages through which they passed. Asked if this was the case on returning, Pte. Porter said no, the people were very quiet and subdued, and did not interfere with them at all. There were 15,000 prisoners at Sennelager - English, Canadians, Indians, Belgians, and French. They had to work hard every day cultivating rough tracts of land. He says their potato crop was fearfully devastated by a sharp frost in early June, and caused great depression among the farmers. They had a paper every day called the `Continental Times' printed in England. This used to give them the `hump' for it always made out the Germans were winning everywhere. All the Germans too, were absolutely confident of winning the war. Several of the German soldiers at Sennelager had lived in England, and there was a great contrast between their friendliness and the `sportiness' of the others. He says he is thankful to get home, but wouldn't have missed the experience for anything. He returns to duty again on the 17th, and hopes to go to the Dardanelles. Mrs. Porter's brother, Pte. R. Rudge, of the 2nd Worcesters, has been missing since a fierce engagement in France some six weeks ago. His home is at Wadborough

(The last part refers to Private 8321 Reginald Rudge, 2nd Battn. Worcestershire Regiment, killed 16th May 1916: no known grave, listed on Le Touret Memorial, Pas de Calais, France. He's from Pirton, listed on the Pirton war memorial)

Private John Pratt   8th Worcesters (Reservist). Lived in New Road. [140926][AL][AV18]
Frederick Preece Lived in High Street [AV18]

Private Leonard Dennis Preece   See Photo  Worcester Regiment. *Evesham Journal, 28 October 1916:* ``PERSHORE MAN WOUNDED. Many in the Pershore District will learn with regret that Pte. Leonard Dennis Preece, of the Worcesters, who only joined the colours last April, is now lying dangerously wounded in a Norwich hospital. Pte Preece is the fourth son of Mr. J.W. Preece, manager for the Pershore Gas Company. Prior to joining the Army, he was clerk to Mr A.E. Baker. He joined the regiment on April 12; in July he went out to France and took part in the battles on the Somme, where he received his injuries in the action with the much-vaunted Prussian Guards. His right thigh was shattered with shrapnel. Pte A Langford, (another Pershore man who has since been killed) saw him in trouble and bound up his wound, and he then crawled into a shell *hole and remained there until the ambulance came along some hours later. His father has been to see him and gives a grave report of his condition. Mr Preece has another son in the Army."*

Private 118771 Frederick Lenox Pritchard listed as 8th Worcesters (territorials) in [AL], absent voters lists put him in Machine Gun Corps. Lived in Bull Entry/Newlands [AV18][AV19] 130

Private John Pritchard 8th Worcesters [EJ141003][AL]

258047 John Pritchard Labour Coy. Lived in Newlands. [AV18][AV19]

Private 63418 George Alfred Pulley, Junr. 6th Worcesters. Lived in Bachelor's Entry [AV18][AV19]

William Quigley Lived at 5 Coventry Terrace [AV18]

Private George Redding 8th Worcesters. Recruited 1914, was 33 years old. Lived in Newlands. [EJ141003][AL]

Captain William Reid A.V.C. Lived in Bridge Street [AV18][AV19]

Private William Reeves [AL] lists him in Kitchener's Army

Evesham Journal 31 July 1915 has an account of Sergt. Biddulph's death, (see Biddulph entry) that lists William's military career. Aged 20, he'd been sent out to the Dardanelles after four months training, and the first battle he was in was the one in which Sergt. Biddulph died (4th June 1915) William was shot in the thigh in that battle, and he returned home wounded at the beginning of July 1915.

Lieut. J. Reid Army Veterinary Corps.

Evesham Journal 8 May 1915:-- ``TOMMY" INCOMPARABLE. Lieut. J. Reid of the Army Veterinary Service, has returned home for a brief period to recuperate. He was veterinary surgeon at Pershore, and joined the army just before Christmas, obtaining shortly afterwards his commission as lieutenant, where he says the ghastly and harrowing scenes he witnessed absolutely baffles description. As brave as are the Germans, and no one with experience, Mr Reid says, can question it, they do not go into the fight with just that avidity or with light-hearted spirit as our men. ``Tommy Atkins" in war is incomparable. Lieut Reid says this very convincingly, although considerably upset that some of the said ``Tommy Atkinses" have relieved him of no less than six Uhlan helmets, which he had with some trouble and not a little danger had secured to bring home as a trophy.

Captain W. Reid Army Veterinary Corps [AL] Evesham Journal 29 July 1916 says he'd been a member of Pershore's hockey club.

Private Albert Richards Kitchener's Army in [EJ140926], 6th Worcesters according to [AL] **A/Sgt 39067 Albert Edward Richards** See Photo Army Service Corps. Lived in Bearcroft. Enlisted

Albert E. Richards

3rd September 1914, working as a baker. Discharged 10 June 1916 from illness. [AV18][AV19] 15 March 1896-25th October 1957. Served in Gallipoli, and was in France in November 1917 (see his brother's entry below)

Private T. Robbins Possibly a Pershore man? Brother in law of H. Stanton [see below]; in June 1916 was in Netley Hospital after serving at the Dardanelles and Mesopotamia.

Sergeant Francis (Frank) Charles Roberts 8th Worcesters [AL] Son of Mr. and Mrs. C.H. Roberts of High Street. [AL] lists him as Lance-Corporal. Went to France with the Territorials at the end of March 1915. Sometime around mid-December 1915 he was injured in the left side with shrapnel wounds.

William Albert Roberts Reservist [EJ140926]; lived High street. Aged 21 when recruited in 1914.

Frank Roberts

326333 John Rock Q.O. Worcs. Hus. Lived in Head Street [AV18][AV19] (AV18 says 5 Coventry Terrace?)

George Rogers Pershore court report, *Evesham Journal 26 August 1916:* - ``A deserter - At the Police Court on Friday afternoon - before

Mr W. Pearce - George Rogers, Batchelor's Entry, was brought up in custody charged with being a deserter from the Army - P.C. Hartford proved the arrest, and defendant was remanded to await a military escort"

Corporal 325529 Thomas Lloyd Roper 1st/1st Q.O.W.H. (Worcestershire Yeo.) d. 9 September 1916 age 20. Son of Thomas and Fanny Roper of Huntley Villa, 31 Westcliffe Drive, Blackpool. (?? but he's the only Roper in the QOWH for the entire war) [AB]

Arthur. Rose Reservist [EJ140926] See Photo

Private 240735 Ernest Rose 2/8th Worcesters. Lived in New Road. Aged 30 when recruited. in 1914 [EJ141003][AL][AV18][AV19] See photo
H.R. Rose Kitchener's Army [EJ140926]

Private 203706 Leonard Rose See Photo 8th Worcesters. Lived in New. Road. [EJ141003][AL][AV18] [AV19] AV19 says he was in 1/7th Worcesters.

Photograph shows the 5 Rose Brothers of New Road who all returned Home from War – Bill, Len, Arthur, Tom and Ern.

Private 82983 Thomas Rose junr. R.A.F. Lived in New Road. AV18][AV19] AV19. See photo

William George Rose Lived in High Street [AV18] See photo

† **200827 Harold Thomas Rose** Worcestershire Regiment 10th Battalion. Born in Pershore killed on 21st March 1918 at Flanders. Enlisted at Kidderminster. Not on Pershore's Roll of Honour.

Herbert Royal Royal Navy [EJ140926][AL]

G. Rudge Reservist [EJ140926]

Sidney William Rutter Lived in Priest Lane [AV18]

Private H. Russell Kitchener's Army [AL]

Gunner William Russell _Evesham Journal 20 February 1915:_-- A TYPICAL ``TOMMY." Gunner William Russell, of the 65th Battery Royal Field Artillery Expeditionary Force, has visited his home at Priest-lane, Pershore, on a few days' leave, but left again on Tuesday for the front. Gunner Russell is the very personification of that sort of ``Tommy Atkins" which this war has revealed, whose amazing sangfroid is the wonder of all nations. A chat with him irresistibly recalled a picture in a recent issue of ``Punch", where a ``tommy" with the inevitable Woodbine in his mouth, and a Uhlan helmet under his arm, is strolling leisurely along a country lane in which is falling a perfect deluge of bursting shells, is accosted by a chum sitting on the road-side, who, his face wreathed in smiles, remarks ``hello Bill! A bit showery 'ere aint it?"

That Gunner Russell has ``been through it" is seen by an ugly shrapnel wound over the left eye, and an arm which he occasionally has to grip until a twinge of pain passes by. And yet, with these reminders of past experiences, and with a certainty of more to come, for he is probably in the trenches by this, he has gone back with as light a heart, as cheerful a face, and as merry an eye as though he were going on a pleasure trip in jolly good company and plenty of cash to spend. Only once did he speak with any gravity: it will be rough on poor mother if I don't come back," he said, which showed he had true manly thoughts for all his indifferent aspects and smiling countenance. It was almost impossible to get him to talk at all about those historic battles of Mons, Marne, Aisne, and La Bassee, in which he had taken part; the chief thing which occupied his mind was an intense desire to try those new big guns which he said the authorities had recently dispatched to France, and which he seemed convinced was infinitely superior to anything the Germans possessed. Asked for his impressions of the German soldiers, he said they were big, powerful fellows, all pale faced, and looking as if they would rather be anywhere but in the firing *line. But one could not call them cowards; they stick at it when they are there. "But," he added, "they are cruel, beastly wretches, officers and men, or they could not have done the things they have." Gunner Russell did not give one much news, but he left an impression of a fine type of the British "Tommy," and we hope his mother will see him back. We should mention that he was three weeks in the hospital at Versailles, from wounds in shoulder and face.*

Percy Sadler Lived in Church Street [AV18]

159673 Edwin Charles Saunders R.F.C. Lived in Priest Lane [AV18][AV19] Brother of Maurice Henry (see below)

265768 Francis Samuel Saunders 3rd. A.M. R.A.F. Lived in Prospect Cottages [AV19]

20402 G. Saunders Worcestershire Regiment - reported as a casualty in Evesham Journal May 13 1916

Lieut. J. Sharp Evesham Journal 29 July 1916 says he'd been a member of Pershore hockey club.

Captain Claude Shelmerdine Evesham Journal 29 July 1916 says this man had been a member of Pershore's hockey club.

Lieut. Neil Shelmerdine According to Evesham Journal 29 July 1916, had been umpire for the Pershore Hockey Club.

Private William George Shepherd Kitchener's Army [AL]
Aged 23 when recruited in 1914. Probably wound up in the same regiment/battalion as Charles Twigg - the 10th Battn. Worcestershire Regiment. By July 1916, he was apparently wounded and out of action. See the letter home in the entry for Charles Twigg.

15631 William George Shepherd 4th Worcesters. Lived in Head Street [AV18][AV19] Possibly same man as previous entry?

Lieutenant C.E. Slater 4th Batt. Royal Warwicks Reserves [EJ140926][AL] [AL] also reports that he was one of those who'd volunteered for service at the front on August 24th 1914.

Evesham Journal 29 July 1916 says he'd been a member of Pershore hockey club

Private Albert Smith   6th Worcesters [AL]

Private 240204 Arthur (Artle) Sydney Smith   1/8th Worcesters. Lived in Victoria Terrace (or Priest lane) Aged 18 when recruited in 1914. [AL][AV18][AV19]

Private 27240 Arthur Thomas Smith 9th Worcesters. Lived Cemetery Lodge. [AV18][AV19]

A. Smith   Reservist [EJ140926]

Private Charles William Smith   Worcesters. Evesham Journal 4th May 1918
ANOTHER PERSHORE MAN A PRISONER. Pte. Charles William Smith, of the Worcesters, son of Mr. And Mrs. Edwin Smith, of the Cemetery House, Pershore, is a prisoner of war in Germany. *About ten days ago the parents received a sympathetic letter from the Commanding Officer, stating that their son was in the firing line on March 25 and had not since been heard of. Mrs. Smith, having seen in the local papers that a list of prisoners was in the possession of Mrs. Wodehouse, Mr. Smith went to Worcester to inspect and found his son's name and number thereon. On Wednesday a postcard was received from Charles, giving his camp address in Germany, and stating that he was all right and so far being well treated. Mr. and Mrs. Smith have another son with the colours in Mesopotamia.*

F. Smith   8th (Home Service) Batt. Worcs. Regt. [EJ141024]

Private George Smith   8th Worcesters [EJ141003][AL]

George Smith Lived in High Street [AV18]

32874 George Frederick Smith   1st Royal Berks Inf. Lived in Bridge Street. [AV18][AV19]. Returned wounded. Was a Postman until he retired.

Rev. Harry Smith *Evesham Journal, 2 January 1915:-- REV. H. SMITH A PRISONER. A good many Pershore people would like to*

hear something definite concerning the Rev. Harry Smith, the eldest son of Mr. J.W. Smith of Pershore, his whereabouts, and how he is faring. It is not many months ago since he was in Pershore, and preached at the Abbey Church. He was then sent out as a delegate of the Universities' Mission to Central Africa to Zanzibar, and as his father had not received the customary communication from him, he wrote to the secretary of the Mission, the Rev. Duncan Travers, at Westminster, and received the following reply:-- ``Dear Mr. Smith. -- Your son is on the mainland and not in Zanzibar. Now the mainland is temporarily cut off and no letters or cables or anything can reach us. We heard that the staff were asked if they would like to move away from the Germans, and they said `No.' There is no danger, but it is of course awkward not being able to communicate. The Bishop is now back in Zanzibar, and he will no doubt do what he can to get in touch with the mainland party''. ``Non-combatants,'' the letter proceeds to state, hardly with justification, ``are secure from molestation, and are sure to be left alone, we think. P.S. Your son went to Magila for a holiday''. In a subsequent communication issued by the Bishop of Zanzibar on November 9, he says: -- ``I seems all our people from Magila have been sent up to Arusha, the German Government station on a hill situate south-west from Kilimanjaro. They are under a German guard.'' So there seem little doubt but what the Rev. Harry Smith is a prisoner. We hope he will soon get released.

Evesham Journal, Nov. 4 1916:-- PERSHORE CLERGYMAN'S RELEASE. The conquest of German East Africa has naturally resulted in the deliverance of many English Prisoners from the unsympathetic hands of the Huns, and among the number is the Rev. H. Smith, the eldest son of Mr. J.W. Smith, of Pershore. Mr. Smith has recently received the welcome news from the Bishop of Zanzibar, and he is now looking forward to the home-coming of his son, whose fate has been a source of anxiety to him ever since the opening days of the war. The Rev. Harry Smith was one of a large party of missionaries sent out to that portion of the Zanzibar diocese, which lies in German East Africa, or rather English East Africa, seeing that now the ownership has changed hands.

From a report issued by the Universities' Mission to Central Africa dated May 31 this year, it appeared that the whole staff was put under arrest directly the war broke out. The harshest treatment, it states, was meted out to the members of the African staff, who were imprisoned in

chains for three weeks then put to hard manual labour of seven days a week, the hardships being so severe that many teachers died under them. The experiences of the European staff (which included the Rev. Smith) were not so hard as this, but were nevertheless very hard to endure. For ten weeks they were imprisoned in an hotel at Lindi, and they were taken back to Masasi for three months, where they were allowed their freedom. On February 20, 1915, they were put under arrest, and had to walk over 400 miles to Morogoro (due west of Dares-Salaam) where they were lodged in a military prison. After five weeks they were taken to another prison, the name of which was censored. It was not until June 11, 1915, that an English mail came to the town where they were imprisoned, and they were allowed to send letters home. All the letters were read by the lieutenant of the prison, and only the briefest messages were allowed. It was then that Mr. Smith received a card from his son with the single line --- `I am well,' which, as welcome as it was, indicated also in a significant manner the despotism that prevailed in that far-off prison. Besides his family, many friends in Pershore will be glad to see the young clergymen again.
Private Hubert Smith   Kitchener's Army [AL]

James William Smith Junr. Lived in High
Street [AV18]

Gunner 248980 William Arthur Smith R.G.A.
See Photo Lived in High Street [AV19]

Pte. H/84105 Alfred Soles 13th Huss. Lived in
Dwelling-house [AV18][AV19]

Private 9811 Frank Soley 1st Worcesters.
Lived in Priest Lane [AL][AV18][AV19]

Evesham Journal, 2 January 1915:-- TWO PERSHORE MEN IN 1ST WORCESTERS. Private F. Soley, of the 1st Worcesters, is invalided home suffering from frostbite in the feet, which he got while in action at La Bassee. He had come over from Egypt, where the regiment had been stationed, and before proceeding to the front, spent a few days at his home in Pershore. He had been out in the fighting line several weeks. He said the Worcesters were in the trenches up to their knees in mud and water, for six nights and five days. fighting at close range, for the enemy was only about twenty yards away. The enemy once made an attempt to rush their position, but they failed. He thought the Worcesters lost about 150, but the German losses must have been enormous. They captured about 300 to 400 Germans. He found his legs very sore, and thought he had rheumatism. They could not take their boots off, for they never knew when they might be attacked. The pain became so great that he at last had to take his boots off, and his feet and legs than started to swell up, and he could not get his boots on again. He had no idea what was the matter with him until he saw the doctor, and he ordered him to the base hospital. For a long time the men had mud frozen on to their boots and putties, and walked, as it were, in leggings. [continued under Charles Grinnell]

Private Fred Soley 15th Hussars [AL]

† **Private 2291 William Harris Somer** Q.O. Worcestershire Hussars (Worcestershire Yeomanry) . Son of John and Jane Somer. Died 24 July 1915 age 39, buried in Alexandria (Chatby) Military and War Memorial Cemetery, Egypt. He's included in this listing because there is a memorial on his parent's grave in Pershore Cemetery, which mentions that his father, John Somer, came from Wadborough. Not listed on the Abbey Memorial. Evesham Journal Roll of Honour 26/9/1914 listed him as Trooper Somer serving in the Yeomanry, under the heading of Pershore (Newtown, Worcester)[EJD16]
Evesham Journal, 31 July 1915 - ``TROOPER W.H. SOMER DROWNED. Ex-Sergt.-Major Somer, Newtown-road, Worcester, has received news that his brother, Trooper William H. Somer, of the Worcestershire Yeomanry, has been drowned near Alexandria, when crossing a river with horses, Trooper Somer was a son of the late Mr. John Somer of Wadborough, near Pershore. He was an excellent horseman and a successful rider at point-to-point meetings in Worcestershire. A telegram has been received from the Commanding Officer of the Worcestershire Yeomanry stating that the death of Trooper W.H. Somer was due to heart failure whilst bathing."*

Private 53028 Arthur Sidney Spalding 1st Somerset Light infantry. Lived at Coventry Terrace [AV19]

2nd.-Lieut. Charles William Spiers East Surreys. Lived in Broad Street [AV18][AV19] Evesham Journal 16 March 1918: ``PERSHORE OFFICERS. Second Lieut. Charles Spiers (son of Mr. Joseph Spiers of Broad Street, Pershore) was gazetted on February 19. He received his training with the Coldstream Guards, and has now joined his regiment, the East Surreys". (rest of article is about G. Stevenson of Wick Post Office)

Evesham Journal October 5 1918: PERSHORE OFFICER WOUNDED. Lieut. Charle s Spiers, of Pershore, is lying in hospital at Rouen, France, wounded in three places -- the face, arms and leg -- caused by a shell bursting. This has been officially reported to the parents, Mr. and Mrs. J. Spiers, of Broad-street. Lieut. Spiers was gazetted to an East Surrey Regiment in January last, and though he had been to France on several occasions he only went into the front line in August last. Before joining up, he was at Messrs. Prothero and Co., grocers, of Broad-street.
210923 Joseph Spiers R.E. (Wireless). Lived in Worcester Street [AV
106666 Clifford Summers M.G.C. Lived Ganderton's row [AV18][AV19]

Gilbert Summers Lived in Ganderton's Row [AV18]

Thomas Charles Summerton Lived at Bearcroft [AV18] 18][AV19]

Private Percy Surman 6th Worcesters [AL]

P. Surman Reservist [EJ140926]

228571 William Robert Tarrant A.S.C. Lived at Victoria Hotel [AV18][AV19]

Arthur William Taylor Lived at High Street [AV18]

Private 32571 James Benjamin Taylor A.V.C. Lived in Dwelling-house [AV18][AV19]

Private John Taylor 8th Worcesters / Reservist. Lived at New Road [EJ140926][AL][AV18] Probably the Jack Taylor that attended Harry Smith's funeral in early 1918.

Private William Taylor Kitchener's Army [AL]

Captain William H. Taylor Evesham Journal 29 July 1916 says this man had been a member of Pershore's hockey club.

Private Alfred Teague 8th Worcesters [AL

Alfred William Teague Lived in Newlands [AV18]
George William Teague Lived in Newlands [AV18]

W. Teague 8th (Home Service) Batt. Worcs. Regt. [EJ141024]
Private 35996 James Ferdinand Teale Garr. Bn. East Yorks.
[AV18][AV19]

Frank Thomas Church Street [AV18]
Private Henry Thomas. Army Service Corps [AL]
Lance Corpl. 24159 Henry Thomas Royal Engineers. Lived in Broad
Street [AV18][AV19]

P.C. Thompson   [EJ140926] listed him as a Reservist, ref [AL] a
couple of months later listed him as 3rd Worcesters - wounded. [AL] in
its review of the year past, says he'd re-joined the Worcestershire
Regiment as a Reservist, and it was reported on 7th October 1914 that
he was lying dangerously wounded in a French hospital.
*Berrow's Journal 10th Oct. 1914 - PERSHORE POLICEMAN
WOUNDED. Police Constable Thompson. who was stationed at
Pershore for 18 months was a reservist in the Worcestershire
Regiment. and he re-joined his regiment at the beginning of the war.
We are sorry to hear that he is in hospital in France dangerously
wounded. On September 1st he wrote from France to Supt. Hill of
Evesham, saying: I am getting on all right, enjoying the best of health,
and am in the highest of spirits. We have not as yet faced our
opponents, but hope to shortly, just to show them what sort of material
they have to contend with.*

*Berrow's Journal, 31 October 1914 - PERSHORE P.C.'s
EXPERIENCES. P.C. Thompson, who is now lying in hospital at
Versailles, was called up on the outbreak of war, being a reservist in
the 3rd Worcesters. In writing to a friend at Pershore he describes his
wounds. One he had through the arm, which is now healing up nicely.
The wound on his leg, it was at first thought, would prove fatal, ``but'',
he says, ``after careful treatment by the doctors I am now going on
fairly well, and can get about a little on crutches. A shrapnel shell
entered his leg just below the knee, and penetrated up the leg to the
top part of the thigh. The doctors are doing all they can to pull me*

through. When it came to the operation, they wished me to have chloroform, but I would not. I stood it fairly well, but afterward wished I had had chloroform. They got a piece of shrapnel out of my leg weighing 3oz. and I am keeping that as a little souvenir" He goes on to say that he was wounded on the 19th September. In speaking of the War, he says ``Our Allied Armies are holding the enemy well in check, while the Russians are playing great havoc with the Germans, and seem to be carrying everything before them. The losses of the Germans must be simply awful" Speaking of the life in hospital, he says: ``We live like fighting cocks, getting four good meals a day, starting with ham and eggs for breakfast, porridge, and all that one's appetite can fancy"

Horace Roughton Tillman Lived in Bridge Street [AV18]

W. Cecil Towers Lived in Bridge Street [AV18]

3986 Albert Charles Townend 1st South Staffords. Lived in Head Street [AV18][AV19]

Private 29961 Charles Arthur Townend 1/7 Worcs. Lived in Head Street [AV18][AV19]

Private H.A. Townend 6th Dragoons [AL]

Private W. Townend Kitchener's Army [AL]

Private Albert Trapp 8th Worcesters [AL]

015557 Alfred Tuck No. 1 Ord. Mobile Heavy Workshops. Lived in Priest Lane [AV18][AV19]

Private 54/093348 Charles Turvey junr. 16th Field Batty., A.S.C. Lived in Newlands. [AV18][AV19]

Henry Samuel Turvey Lived in Bridge Street [AV18]

Cpt 30071 Robert Turvey Royal Warks. Lived in High Street [AV18][AV19]

Private W. Turvey 8th Worcesters [EJ141003][AL]

240730 William Turvey junr. 9th Worcesters Lived in Head Street [AV18][AV19]

† **Private 21285 Horace Henry/Henry Twigg** - 1st Battalion Prince Albert's (Somerset Light Infantry) Baptised at Pershore Holy Cross on 22 January 1896, the son of William and Ann Twigg of the Newlands. Died 15 July 1916. Soldiers Died in the Great War says he came from Pershore, but enlisted at Bristol. Died of wounds: theatre of war: `home' Buried in Bristol (Greenbank Cemetery, Glos., ref. Green E.365) Not listed on Abbey memorial; listed in the Somerset regiment memorial book as coming from Pershore.

Private George Tye Coldstream Guards. Returned home 19 September 1914; first man to arrive back home; wounded by shrapnel in his foot at the battle of Mons. Lived in Head Street. (Pershore almanac 1915)

Berrow's Worcester Journal, 19th September 1914:-- PERSHORE MAN'S STORY. An interesting narrative has been given to our Pershore correspondent by a Private of the Coldstream Guards, who is invalided home with a shrapnel wound in the foot. Speaking about the battle of Mons, he said the Guards had been marching for about 19 hours on the Saturday. They took up a position on the Saturday evening, acting as a reserve for the firing line. The fighting continued at dawn on the Sunday morning. The 5th brigade had a fall back, and retired through the Guards' trenches. Shrapnel fire from the enemy became so hot that they had to clear out. They retired from Mons, fighting their way to Landrecies, where they billeted in the village.
After a short rest, an alarm was sounded, and they had to turn out. They had been surprised by the enemy in the dark. It was in this surprise engagement that this Guardsman, who had taken part in two engagements previously, was bowled over. It was seen that the enemy was in vastly superior numbers ``That was the only thing they had got in their favour", said the soldier, `For they have got no fight in them. The bayonet is the thing they `gib' at. I am glad to say some of the Black Country go at them with the bayonet, and they were only too pleased to do so. After that engagement we left about 800 or 900 in the village. The pluck of the officers was splendid".
``CHRISTMAS DINNER IN BERLIN." It made one's heart bleed to see the French and Belgian peasants hurrying along the roads seeking shelter anywhere and leaving behind homes, perhaps in flames, or

demolished in other ways. I was sent home to Netley Hospital, where I spent 14 days. I came to Pershore on Friday last [11th September?] on a 14 days' furlough, as my wife is staying here. I shall soon be well again, and I hope then to be sent back to the fighting line, where I hope to pay with interest for the wound I got. I look back on what has taken place as a hideous nightmare, but I want to get back again, and have only got one wish now, that I may have my Christmas dinner served out to me in Berlin" In conclusion, he paid high tribute to the great kindness shown to the British troops by the Frenchmen, who always appear to have a plentiful supply of tobacco.

William Bradforth Walker Lived at The Chestnuts [AV18]

Private 29220 Charles Walters Oxford and
Bucks. Light Infantry. Lived in Head Street
[AV18][AV19]

Private 236191 Alfred Ward See Photo 1st/1st
Bn. Herefordshire regiment d. 13th November
1920 age 31. Son of William and Annie Ward;
husband of Blanch Ward of Church Street. Born in
Pershore. CWGC grave in Pershore Cemetery.
[AV18][AV19]

Captain Watson Evesham Journal 26 May 1917 - `
.so well remembered in Pershore for his services in
connection with the Territorial Forces, has been awarded the Military
Cross"

Corporal H. Wedgebury Listed in Evesham Journal, 30 June 1917
amongst those on the Pershore Post Office Roll of honour, described
as missing, believed killed.

Private Fred Wells. 8th Hussars [AL]

Pte. H/325543 Reginald White 1/1/ Worcs. Yeomanry. Lived in Bridge
Street [AV18][AV19]

101709 Charles Christopher Wilks 16th Sqd. M.G.C. Lived in High
Street [AV18][AV19]

Trooper Christopher C. Wilks Worcs. Yeomanry [AL]

Percy Wilks 2nd City of Birmingham Battalion [AL]
52750 Percival John Wilks 9th Manchesters. lived in High street [AV18][AV19]

193161 Leonard Bayfield Willcox Royal Garrison Artillery. Lived at Bachelor's Entry [AV18][AV19]

Corpl. 485382 Bertram William Jameson Williams Labour Cps. Lived in York Cottages [AV18][AV19]

M/334851 Leonard Williams A.S.C., M.T. Lived in Little Priest Lane [AV18][AV19]

Pte. 93467 Walter Thomas Williams Duke of Cornwall's L.I. Lived in York Cottages [AV18][AV19]

Ralph Willis Lived in High Street [AV18]

Thomas Henry Frederick Willis Lived in High Street [AV18]

Corporal Edward Winwood Kitchener's Army. Lived in Priest Lane [AL][AV18]

Private 13164 Ernest Witts 10th Hants. Lived at Tiddesley Wood [AV18][AV19]

G. Witts Kitchener's Army [EJ140926]
94650 Harry Witts 158 Labour Coy. Lived at Tiddesley Wood [AV18][AV19]

Private 13184 James Andrew `Jack' Witts 12th Hants. Lived at Tiddesley Wood [AV18][AV19] Listed twice in AV19, refs. 5371 and 4768

Private John Witts Kitchener's Army [EJ140926][AL

Squadron Sergeant-Major Frank Wood See Photo Worcs. Yeomanry. Evesham Journal 27th

February 1915 has coverage of the wedding of Warrant Officer Frank Wood of Pershore. [AL][EJ140926] Sergt. Major Wood had been a member of Pershore hockey club, according to Evesham Journal 29 July 1916

W. Wood Reservist [EJ140926]

Private William Wood Royal Field Artillery [AL]

William Wood Lived at Knight's Buildings [AV18]

William Frank Bomford Wood Lived in Little Priest Lane [AV18]

Private Arthur Workman 5th Lancers [AL]

Private Henry Workman Kitchener's Army [AL]

Private 4/97366 Henry Workman 627 Ag. co. Labour Corps [AV19]

John James Workman Lived in High Street [AV18]

Lance-Corporal 17886 John Workman 11th Worcs. Lived in Priest Lane [AV19]

Private Joseph Workman Kitchener's Army [AL]

190113 William James Workman Royal Engineers. Lived in The Ryde [AV18][AV19]

Corporal M/323277 Alfred Charles Wright A.S.C. Lived in Newlands ([AV18]) or Priest Lane ([AV19])

Pte. 94659 Arthur Wright 158 Lab. Coy. Lived in No Gains [AV18][AV19]

Private Archibald Young 8th Worcesters [AL]

Private Fred Young 8th Worcesters [AL]

Frederick Archibald Young Lived at Bachelor's Entry [AV18]

G. Young Kitchener's Army [EJ140926]
44218 George Arthur Victor Young Cavalry Reserves. Lived at Knight's Buildings [AV18][AV19]

Private John Young. Kitchener's Army [AL]

Gunner 17800 John Henry Young R.G.A. Lived at 22 High Street [AV18][AV19]

27146 Walter Young Dorsets. Lived at Bachelor's Entry [AV18][AV19]

PERSHORE WAR MEMORIAL.

This photograph was taken by local photographer Joseph Glover of Pershore taken on the first Armistice Day (11th November 1921) after the memorial had been unveiled. The formal Dedication Ceremony took place in Pershore Abbey on Tuesday 1st November 1921 at 3pm where the memorial was unveiled by the 9th Earl of Coventry.

The memorial was designed by Alfred Drury, RA. who has inscribed his name on the terrestrial sphere.

Photograph kindly donated by Eileen Skidmore who found it in her Grandmother's scrap book.

Visit Pershore Abbey's website at:
http://www.pershoreabbey.org.uk/

.

*Photograph courtesy
of Andrew Burge*

Some other local men ...

Lieutenant Alban John Benedict HUDSON

Age: 23
Born in Headington, Oxfordshire in July 1893 –
not on Pershore's War Memorial. "B" Company,
3rd Battalion Worcestershire Regiment formerly
"A" Company, 11th Battalion. Killed in action on
7th June 1917 at Flanders. Buried Lone Tree
Cemetery (Spanbroekmolen), Wijtschate,
West-Vlaanderen, Belgium. Grave Ref:
I. B. 1. Commoner of Magdalen College, Oxford.
Commemorated at Malvern Priory, Worcestershire, and in the parish
church of St. Mary, Wick, Worcestershire, also in the Chapel of Wyke
Manor, Pershore, Worcestershire.

Alban's parents later moved in to Wick Manor where an alabaster
monument in the form of a recumbent effigy of Alban on a quatrefoiled
tomb chest was installed in the Chapel.

**Nephew of Alfred Henry Hudson of Wick Manor, Wick, Pershore -
cousin of Aubrey & Arthur Hudson
Son of Rev & Mrs C H Bickerton Hudson of Holy Rood , St Giles,
Oxford and later of Wyke Manor, Wick, Pershore.**

Evesham Journal 16th June 1917 – PERSHORE AND THE WAR

*"The little village of Wick, which has sent practically all her eligible sons to the
war, many of whom, alas, will never return, sorrows again to learn of the
death in action of Lieut. Alban Hudson, who was so well known to the villages
by his frequent visits before the war to his second cousin, Colonel A H Hudson,
Wick House. This fine young officer was the only son of the Rev. C Bickerton
Hudson of Oxford, who has considerable land and property possessions in
Wick. The deceased belonged to the Worcester and was killed in a recent
action in France. In the early months of the war he was billeted in Worcester
some time with Captain Warren Hudson ,who is now a Major, and in
commence of a labour battalion. Seldom an important battle takes place in
this mighty war but the Worcesters are in it and with the Worcesters of
course are the majority of the Pershore men. The Roll of Honour which is*

attached to the door of the old Abbey Church gets larger and larger and now assumes considerable proportions.

Captain Frank Hutchinson Kennedy
(See Photo)
Royal Army Medical Corps.
Came to Pershore as a G.P.
in the 1920's and lived
here until he died in 1974.
He was present at the Battle
of the Somme.

Sapper Enoch PEART Service No 252404
(See Photo) 367th Forestry Company Royal
Engineers Died aged 33 of Influenza on 5th
December 1918 Son of Enoch and Mary Peart, of
Great Comberton; Husband of Edith Peart, of
Great Comberton, Pershore,Served four years in
France.Buried in Janval Cemetery, Dieppe,
France, Grave I. ZZ. 5.appears on: Great
Comberton War Memorial Great Comberton St
Michael's Church individual plaque:

Sapper E. PEART,
Royal Engineers
(Died.)

**IN LOVING MEMORY OF MY DEAR
HUSBAND ENOCH PEART,
PRIVATE 1ST BATTALION
WORCESTERSHIRE REGIMENT,
AFTER 4 YEARS SERVICE
HE DIED AT DIEPPE, FRANCE,
DEC: 5, 1918, AGED 33 YEARS.**
"In due season we shall reap if we faint not."

Charles Stewart STEVENSON *(see photo)*
Service No: 7807
Age 31
Killed in action 31st October 1914
Buried in Ration Farm Military Cemetery,
La Chapelle-D'Armentieres, France, Grave
VII. A. 20. Appears on: Wick St Mary's Church
Memorial in Pershore Working Men's Club
**Son of Mr & Mrs T H Stevenson of Wick Post Office,
Nr Pershore.**

Sgt C Stevenson of Wick Post Office -31 years

Evesham Journal – 5th December 1914 DEATH OF SERGEANT CHARLES STEVENSON

Sergeant Charles Stevenson, fourth son of Mr & Mrs T H Stevenson of Wick Post Office, near Pershore was recently killed in action. The sad intelligence was tersely transmitted to the parents from the War Office accompanied by Lord Kitchener's black edged letter expressing the sympathy of the King and Queen. The place where he met his death was not stated.

Sergeant Stevenson, who was in the 2nd Essex Regiment, 12th Infantry 5th Division commonly known as "Pompadours" had come unscathed through several of the hottest engagements of this great war. His last letter to his Mother, received not so many days before the news came of his death, said "We are billeted in a small village after the worst day we had since we came out. Luckily, very luckily, I have again escaped being hit. Nearly all my platoon got killed or wounded in the last fight. I only have 16 men left out of 45. My officer got killed. The Germans tried to break through but we stopped 'em." The tone of the whole letter was in contrast to previous ones in which he wrote light-heartedly and jokingly. This was written just following a fierce struggle to which he alluded and it was evident he was depressed by the loss of so many of his comrades.

From the second despatch of General Sir John French it is clear that the regiment in which Charlie Stevenson was sergeant was engaged in that memorable fight at the wood of Compiegne in the retreat from Mons where the famous Prussian Guards, the pride of the German Army, were shattered and decimated in their vain attempts to overpower the "thin red line" of the British Infantry.

Sergeant Stevenson is the second representative of the little village of Wick who has died while fighting for his country. The first, as need hardly be recalled, for his death occasioned such sadness as will take a long lapse of time to modify, was Lieutenant Aubrey Hudson who fell in one of the very first skirmishes of the war on French territory.

Sergeant Stevenson, who was just 31 years of age, had served nine years as a soldier in this same regiment, the 22nd Essex. He was a fine type of soldier; he looked it, he loved the life, was thoroughly suited to it and was destined, we believe, to make a success of it. He was widely known and popular in the neighbourhood of his home. In his youth, he was apprenticed for five years in the ironmongery business of the late Mr C H Field of Pershore. He went from Pershore to Ingatestone in Essex to an ironmongery firm there and it was while her that he enlisted.

Much sympathy is felt for the parents in the loss they are now feeling most acutely. Three other sons of Mr & Mrs Stevenson are serving their country – Glennis Stevenson, who at the outbreak of war left a good position at Rempston Hall near Loughborough and is already a Lance-Corporal in the Sherwood Foresters; Thomas Stevenson who is a Petty Officer on board his Majesty's ship Argonaut (he has been 12 years in the Navy) and James Stevenson in Canada who immediately allied himself to the Canadian Volunteer forces. Another son, George who served in the Berkshire Yeomanry through the Boer war and has four clasps, is only deterred from joining the Army by Doctor's orders.

The Father, Mr T H Stevenson of Wick had a most adventurous life abroad. He is an ex-Sergeant of the Artillery, has been a transport officer in the Malay States in the Chinese Revenue Service and served for many years under the Indian Government as a qualified sanitary inspector, also holding the responsible post of Superintendency of Conservancy. He was a transport officer in the Malay States during the Pabrang Rebellion. He and Mrs Stevenson lived for some time in China.

Evesham Journal
5th September 1914

DRILL AT PERSHORE.

The National Reservists of Pershore still continue to drill twice weekly, and last Sunday's operations in the hockey ground were witnessed by Lord Coventry, Lord Deerhurst, Capt. J. B. Dowson, and Lieut. Hugh Davies. Between 50 and 60 men were present, and Lord Coventry presented to about half the number the badges of the National Reserve. In doing so his Lordship spoke of the progress of the war, England's justification for entering the field, and of the necessity of determinedly prosecuting the war until our enemies, who had so shamefully disregarded the honour of international treaty, were beaten and humiliated. His Lordship further added that he hoped the patriotism of the Pershore Reservists would stimulate many young fellows to offer themselves for their country. The men were drilled by Major F. Checketts, and Messrs. Murphy and Dyer. Among the Reservists was Mr. J. H. Smyth, of Fladbury Manor, who last week was sworn in as Commander of the Fladbury and District Special Constables. Recruiting has not been very flourishing in the Pershore district, but now the harvest is beginning to wane, young men are coming forward in a far more gratifying manner. Mr. Hugh Mumford, of the Three Springs, who served in Paget's Horse in the South African campaign, has again volunteered for active service, and has left Pershore some few days since.

Mr. W. Wood, hon. secretary of the Pershore Steeplechase Committee, has sent a cheque for ten guineas to the Prince of Wales' Fund, on behalf of the committee. At Throckmorton Church last Sunday, at the close of a sermon on the war by the Rev. D. K. Sylvester, a collection taken for the Prince of Wales's Fund realised £1 4s. The school children of Throckmorton have voluntarily foregone their annual summer treat, and asked that the money collected for it should go to the war fund.

PERSHORE'S LOCAL COMMITTEE FOR WAR DISTRESS.

A meeting of this committee was held at the Board Room, Pershore, on Tuesday after the meetings of the Board of Guardians and District Council. Those present were the members of the District Council. On the proposition of Mr. Dee, Mr. T. W. Parkes was elected chairman and on Mr. Parkes' motion, Mr. A. E. Baker was appointed secretary, the question of remuneration to be left over. It was agreed to co-opt the local secretaries of the Soldiers' and Sailors' Families Association as members of the committee and also the local superintendent of the Prudential Assurance Company. An executive committee was appointed and other business transacted.

Evesham Journal
12th September 1914

Evesham Journal Archives 12th September 1914:   PERSHORE

A meeting promoted by Messrs H Basil Harrison and W Wood, Chairmen respectively of St Andrew and Holy Cross Parish Councils, took place at the Music Hall on Tuesday night for the purpose of giving a stimulus to recruiting. The meeting was remarkable for its size, its enthusiasm and its results. The hall was packed to the doors, many being unable to find admission and the spirit of patriotic fervour animated speaker and hearers alike. Lord Deerhurst presided and with him on the platform were Lady Deerhurst, Hon Helena Deerhurst, Major-General Frank Davies, Admiral Cummings, Revs. H F Peile (Archdeacon Warwick), F R Lawson (rector of Fladbury), Rev Harcourt Fowler (Vicar of Elmley Castle), Col. A H Hudson, Miss Hudson, Capt. And Mrs Derrington Bell, Miss Bell, Mr & Mrs O Wynne Marriott, Major F Checketts, Capt. J B Dowson, Der Emerson, Messrs G F Hooper, T W Parkes, J E Newman etc. In the front row of chairs sat an old Crimean veteran – Mr Lewis of Fladbury – whose presence and bearing compelled attention. Deafening cheers broke from the audience when Lord Deerhurst invited him on the platform and introduced him. He is as fine a looking old soldier as one would meet anywhere. Tall and of massive proportions, with leonine heat and profile, his great chest being adorned with medals declaring him to have been a unit of the old 46th Duke of Cornwall's Light Infantry whose exploits in the trenches before Sebastopol added much to the glory of our Army's history.

It is due to the patriotism of Pershore and the villages immediately surrounding it to mention here a fact which was not brought out at the meeting, which is that the men who now joined up brought up the number of recruits for the past three weeks to well over a hundred (exclusive of Fladbury, 38) and that these when added to the Territorials, Yeomanry and independents already gone up to a splendid total of 300. Every day they come in, young fellows of brawn and muscle, hard as nails and fit as fiddles from their daily toil in the field and garden, the very chaps that should develop into the finest British Soldiers.

Lord Deerhurst commenced by saying that the war was due to the arrogance and greed of an individual who not only wanted to be Emperor of his own domain, but also the whole of Europe. The Kaiser was madly jealous of our wealth and possessions but what England had, she was going to keep and there were hundreds, thousands, aye millions, who were willing to lay down their lives for the old flag of Great

Britain and to thwart the wicked designs of this military despot (Cheers). Lord Kitchener wanted the men to make the issue of this campaign an absolute certainty and it was up to the men of England, who alone of the great powers adopted and maintained the principle of voluntary service, to now come forward in the time of their country's great need (Applause).

In the fine speech of Admiral Cummings which followed, he spoke of England's justification for entering on war, the heroic stand of plucky Belgium and the shameful, disgraceful behaviour of the Germans instancing the destruction of Louvaine.

Major –General Frank Davies, who had a great reception, also made a stirring speech. "History" he said "repeated itself". Once again this country was fighting for the freedom of Europe. A hundred years ago, we were at war against one of the greatest soldiers of the world's history; now we were out to crush the greatest military power that ever flaunted itself. But a century ago, we were not united and many took the side of the enemy. Today, however, the Empire stood solidly as one, irrespective of creed, nationality or colour (Cheers). He knew Germany, had been there a good deal and knew its language. He had many friends there, some in the army. As soldiers, they had no quarrel with the men they had to fight. He believed the German nation at heart was kindly desirous of the pursuit of peace. It was the caste that ruled them, the caste that made war their God. They hated our wealth, they hated our freedom, they intended to put us down. France was to be crushed first and then their ports on the other side of the Channel would have been utilised against England. Anybody who wanted to know what it would be like to be ruled by Germany could read it in the blood-stained annals of Belgium. Poor little Belgium. What had she done? Simply sought to uphold her treaty rights, granted by whom? By Germany itself. The Bully (Cheers and a voice: They will have their gruel yet"). "Yes" concluded the speaker. "Germany hang 'em; they were out to smash us but by God, they shan't do it." The blunt military manner of the General worked the audience up to a tremendous enthusiasm.

Mr Parkes who followed, describing the conflict as a fight for the freedom of civilisation and expressing the opinion it would be the last war we or our children would see. A powerful entreaty to young men to come forward was emphasised by the recital of Nelson's motto never more applicable, commented the speaker than now: "England expects that every man this day will do his duty". The bright streak in the present crisis, continued Mr Parks, was the splendid co-operation of all the classes. There was no creed, no politics, no social distinction. We were all Britishers. It was therefore with a feeling of repulsion that he read in the local evening paper a letter – a small, mean, nonsensical letter trying to cause some political discussion. "Shame on the man who wrote it" cried Mr Parkes amid cheers.

No one trounced the "unscrupulous originator" of the war more than Col. Hudson in his vigorous ten minutes' speech. The Colonel emphasised the fact that our Government had used every possible means of conciliation to maintain peace and that war was provoked by Germany, regardless of sacred treaties and obligations, and for the sole purpose of satisfying their avaricious greed for territory. He alluded to Mr Asquith's magnificent oration at the Guildhall as befittingly expressing the sentiments of Englishmen.

The Ven. Archdeacon of Warwick said we were at war for the sacredness of treaty obligations and for the plighted troth of the English people also. Shame upon them – of the Germans as well. Had we been fools enough to acquiesce in their innocent arrangements, they would, in all probability, have secured naval bases on the English Channel. The Archdeacon paid a splendid tribute to our magnificent Army and Navy.

Other fine speakers , each of which found great acceptance with the audience were made by the Rev F R Lawson, Mr J E Newman and Mr J Cooke, the popular recruiting Sergeant for Pershore and a splendid meeting concluded by the lusty singing of three verses of the National Anthem, led by Mr Charles Mason, the Abbey Organist.

Evesham Journal archives 14th November 1914
– REFUGEES AT PERSHORE

Great interest was shown by the townspeople in the arrival of the first batch of Belgian refugees. They came to Laughern House in Bridge Street, the residence recently purchased by Mr J R Lacy, a Birmingham Solicitor, who not only has granted free use of the spacious premises but also is generously providing for their maintenance. The furniture has mostly been lent by townspeople and the house is adequately and comfortably furnished for the accommodation of the visitors. Mrs Arthur Baker, with the assistance of Miss A Matthews, has kindly consented to supervise the catering arrangements. Flags were put up at some of the houses in the street and a crowd awaited their arrival and greeted them with cheers. The refugees were conveyed from Defford Station at five o'clock in the evening in Mr Burnham's motor cars. Among those who went to meet them were the Rev. Father Norman Holly of Pershore (who has also arranged to put up at his own house a Belgian journalist and his son and a Flemish priest), Mr J R Lacy, Mrs Morris and Messrs J G Baker, A E Baker, P Hanson and W Lloyd. The visitors numbered eighteen altogether with the addition of three sisters to look after them. Mother Gouzaage, Mother Ignatious and Sister Bernadittr. This trio speak English excellently and will doubtless be of great assistance. They came from Thelderic, near Romaines and Malines. The refugees are three families and number 18. They are sent by the Catholic Women's League. They are mostly of the fisher type and hail from Ostend. At the siege, they were cast adrift in a sailing boat and were on the water twenty-four hours being picked up by a sailing boat and brought to Folkestone.

Evesham Journal 1914

On Tuesday last 259 soldiers from Worcester on a route march chose Pershore as the object of a visit for the purpose of giving a stimulus to recruiting. It was Captain Warren Hudson's Company of one of the new battalions of the Worcesters. A splendid lot of fellows of fine physique and bearing, they swung into the town to the lilt of their own music, the singing of "Tipperary", "We are the Worcester Boys" and other such-like lyrics. After parading and drilling in the Broad Street before a large and admitting crowd, the men adjourned to lunch, part going to the Royal Three Tuns, part to the Angel Hotel and the officers to Wick House by kind invitation of Col. A. H. Hudson, father of Capt. Warren Hudson.

One of the other officers with the company was Second-Lieutenant Alban Hudson, son of the Rev. C H Bickerton Hudson. On the afternoon of the visit and since then, several local young men have enlisted making the percentage for Pershore over 7% of the population.

RECRUITING MORE MEN - THE DERBY SCHEME

By Spring 1915, the number of volunteers joining up was dwindling to an average of 100,000 a month which could not be sustained. In an effort to find a way to recruit more men without bringing in full conscription, the Derby Scheme was introduced by the Government. It was named after the originator of the idea Edward Stanley, 17th Earl of Derby and the Government passed the National Registration Act on 15th July 1915. All men not already in the military between the ages of 15 and 65 were obliged to register and give their employment details. By September 1915, the figures were available and showed that there were approximately 5 million males of military age with 1.6 million of these *starred as being in a protected, high or rare skilled job.

Lord Derby was made Director General of Recruiting on 11th October 1915 and introduced the "Derby Scheme" which ran from 16th October until 12th December 1915. Many recruitment offices were so overwhelmed with numbers of men that medical examinations were dispensed with on the basis that they would be medically examined once they were called up for service. Men who attested to the scheme would be paid one day's wages, placed in B Class Army Reserve then released back to their civilian lives until the military called them up. To identify these men, they were given a khaki armband. Men who attested to the scheme were still able to volunteer for military service if they weren't called up under the Derby Scheme. Nearly 50% of the men attesting to the scheme did so between 10th & 13th December 1915 - 1,070,478 men.

On 20th December 1915, Lord Derby made the following report to Parliament which outlined that 5,011,441 men were available for enlistment, 2,950,514 had attested, enlisted or tried to enlist and 2,060,927 had not attested, enlisted or tried to enlist. Out of the 5,011,441 men available for service, only 59% attempted to register for military service with 275,000 (5%) enlisted for immediate service and 9% of the available men rejected.

The first call up notice was announced this day for groups 2, 3, 4 and 5 (single men aged 19 to 22) to take effect from January 1916. Groups 6, 7, 8, and 9 (single men aged 23 to 26) were given notice on 8th January 1916 to be called up on 8th February 1916.

At the same time, Parliament were still discussing conscription and this led to the Home Secretary resigning on 31st December 1915. Conscription would involve forcibly attesting all eligible men who were not already serving or attesting under the Derby Scheme. The Derby scheme ran again from 10th January 1916 until the Military Service Act on 1st March 1916 conscripted every eligible man, not already either serving or a member of the Class B army reserve into the Class B reserve.

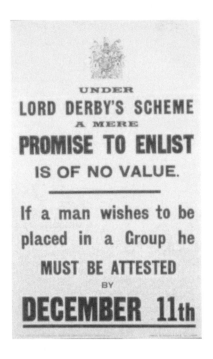

WHITE FEATHERS

At the start of the war in August 1914, Admiral Charles Fitzgerald founded the Order of the White Feather with support from prominent women, Feminists and Suffragettes. The organisation encouraged women to present men not in military uniform with a white feather as a sign of cowardice so as to persuade them to join up.

In 1915, the campaign gathered pace with the perception that there were large manpower shortages in the military. The campaign was not popular amongst Soldiers as even they, at home at leave out of uniform, were on the receiving end of these feathers. Also public and civil servants found likewise and therefore the Government's response was to authorise the production of a badge "for King and Country" to mark out the wearer as somebody effectively excluded from overt pressure to enlist.

For many on the receiving end of these feathers, the shame was too much and they were bullied into enlisting. Some were lads too young to enlist and lied about their age. Some pacifists were more philosophical. Fenner Brockway claimed that he had enough feathers now to make a fan!

CONSCRIPTION

The Military Service Act was introduced in January 1916 meant that every single man aged 18-45 had to join up unless they were widowed with children or religious ministers. In June 1916, this Act was extended to include married men too. Men could appeal against conscription via a local Military Tribunal on health, employment or religious grounds. The latter became known as Conscientious Objectors and approximately 6000 of them were imprisoned. The Military Service Act was amended several times and the age limit was increased to 51. This is the record of one session of Military Tribunal hearings for Pershore. As you will read, many employers were left without skilled workers as the demand for new recruits grew:

PERSHORE RURAL - Several Military Appeals
Berrow's Journal 2nd December 1916

Thursday. Present: Messrs J Faulkner (Chairman), A A Paull, J W Dee, M Revill, G Eccles, W Wood and J Watson, Mr E C Cholmondeley (Military Representative) Mr F Davies (Agricultural Representative)

The Military applied for a review of the case of Charles Arnold Crapp, single), auctioneer and general manager of the Pershore Co-operative Fruit Market but a note was received from Col. Miller Recruiting Officer than instructions had been received from the War Office that the appeal should be withdrawn.

Sidney J Sharp, miller (34) married, no children, partner with his brother Harry in the working of Wyre Mills, Pershore was represented by Mr J S Pritchett, Barrister of Birmingham, in an appeal by the Military Authorities against the conditional exemption already granted. Mr Sharp claimed his work was of skilled character and of national important, especially at the present time, and that he was in a certified occupation. He said if he went the mill would have to be shut up. The Military had offered no substitute. He and his brother worked the mill entirely themselves. They did a good deal of grinding for farmers, averaging 4000 bushels a year and supplied a good deal of feeding stuffs. They expected to be even more busy in view of the new Government regulations respecting standard flour. The old stone mills could deal better with the new kind of flour than the roller mills. The Tribunal decided to refuse the Military Appeal.

Joseph Glover (41) photographer, shopkeeper etc. asked for his application to be heard in private. His previous appeal was dismissed but his appeal before the County Tribunal was referred back to Pershore. Conditional exemption was now granted.

Harry Taylor (35) single, a Kempsey Farmer of 200 acres, whose temporary exemption expired on the 1st, made application for conditional exemption. His brother Norman (23) his stockman had been exempted. Applicants request was granted on the condition that if a substitute was found the younger brother joined. Mr Cholmondeley said if Norman did not pass the medical test, he should appeal for a revision of this case.

Having found as they claimed a substitute for Arthur James Bennett (26) single, shepherd and assistant cowman for Mr C Hewlett, former of Birlingham, the Military asked for the certificate to be cancelled. Mr Hewlett said the substitute was recommended to him as a good man but from enquires he found he had not been accustomed to milk cows or look after sheep. Applicant had at present 104 ewes, 86 cattle and frankly he did not like the idea of parting with an experienced and very reliable man for one whom he knew nothing about, neither ought to be expected to do so. Mr Davies said he thought the Military did not realise the extreme importance of experienced shepherds.

He understood the substitute would be given a week's trial before the man whose place he was to take was withdrawn. Mr Dee: A good general farm hand. And he has worked on the roads for the Upton

District Council. Military appeal refused. Certificate already granted to be altered to April 1.

Rowland Oliver Rose (36), single, of Cropthorne said he had been passed for sedentary work at home. He worked seven acres of garden land single-handed and helped everybody in his parish who wanted him. Conditional.

The Military applied for the conditional exemption granted to Walter Harold Harris, plumber and engineer of Broad Street, Pershore to be cancelled. Harris said he was married and worked for his Father who at present was very ill in Malvern. They had only one labourer working for them now. Seven men had left and joined the Army. In addition to the plumbing business they had nine acres of grass land and kept three cows, two horses and nine pigs. He had been passed for general service. Mr Paull: the Doctors appear to pass anybody nowadays. Mr Cholmondeley, referring to an invitation issued to the medical officers at Norton Barracks to any member of Tribunals to go up and see how the work was done, asked Mr Paull why he did not go. Mr Paull said that he had not the time. Mr Revill said he should take care to stop away for fear they might "collar" him. Military appeal allowed.

The Military also asked for Archibald Bowkett (31) single, market gardener, Defford. He had 8.5 acres and half an acre was open. He had been passed for garrison duty abroad but would sooner stop at home. Appeal allowed.

Mr Roberts, Solicitor, Evesham represented James Teale (28), married, no children, a wardrobe dealer, oilman and carter for the Pershore Co-operative Market and R T Smith and Co. The Military asked for the certificate to be withdrawn. Mr George Daniels, a Lieutenant in the local Fire Brigade, supported the claim that the exemption should stand as Teale was one of the best firemen the Brigade had now to rely upon. Mr Cholmondeley asked Teale why he had told the Recruiting Officer he would be willing to serve on December 1st. Applicant replied because he had been misled. After he obtained his exemption the Military pressed him as to serving and he discovered afterwards that the Tribunal who granted the exemption was the only body who could take it from him. The Military appeal was allowed by Mr Cholmondeley granted the request of the Tribunal that he should not be called up before January 1st.

Joseph Evans (31), married, no children, Pershore was appealed for by the Military Mr Cholmondeley said a substitute had been offered to and accepted by Mr D Tower, the employer. Evans said his employer had been waiting outside for some time as he wanted to know what sort of substitute he was likely to get (laughter) but he had now gone home. He had worked for Mr Tower for seven years on his garden plantation on the Hill. Certificate withdrawn providing an efficient substitute was provided. Mr Cholmondeley said that he would like it to read "Provided a substitute be found to the satisfaction of the Board of Agriculture Representative" in order to find that gentleman something to do (Laughter). Mr Davis intimated he was not desirous of the job

Berrow's Journal 1914
PERSHORE WOMEN VOLUNTEERS
"Enthusiastic Meeting"

A meeting was held at the Masonic Hall, Pershore, on Tuesday evening for the purpose of forming a branch of the Women's Volunteer Reserve. A large number of ladies attended, Col. Miller presided and he was supported by Mrs Smithett (Organising Secretary of London who was the speaker). Mrs Henderson (County Branch Secretary) Mrs Hopkins (Birmingham Organising Secretary for the Midlands) and Miss M Davies and Miss G Hudson (Pershore). The two last-named ladies are to act as Joint Local Secretaries. Col A H Hudson was also present. The meeting was very enthusiastic although comparatively few ladies gave their names. It is expected that more will join when the time comes for drill. The movement is to train and discipline a band of women so that they may be ready to act in any emergency and to provide co-operation among women, improve their physique and teach them to help others. Colonel Miller gave a rousing speech on the object of the movement. Colonel Miller said at a time like the present, they all felt that they wanted to do something for the good of the nation and to help in this time of war. That movement would be the means of setting men free. The women would be of great use in signalling and in various other ways. In the event of invasion, there would be great work for them and they would find that instead of a general panic they would each know what to do.

Mrs Smithett said the movement had been considerably extended of late and she foresaw that Pershore was going to be amongst the places to come forward in a large body. The work was varied and it was most extraordinary the way the branches had developed. The members found from experience that they derived great benefit physically and it gave everyone an occupation. They all felt the great need of doing something for England. The age for joining was from 18 years to 50 years and she suggested to the local Secretaries that if there was a desire to join on the part of any under the age of 18 then a cadet corps should be formed. After the war was over, they had every intention of continuing the movement. The work which could be done was camp cooking, signalling, first aid and various other things. There was always the possibility of an air raid and if such should come about there would be no panic on the part of the members of the WVR. There was some doubt existing as to whether members of the Volunteer Aid Detachment would join the WVR. She pointed out that they were most pleased to welcome them as members (applause).

Miss M Davies of Elmley Castle stated that drills would be held at the gymnasium on Tuesdays at 5pm and Fridays at 7pm and that drills would commence on Friday next when any who wished to join could do so then. She also extended an invitation to any who did not wish to join but who took an interest in the movement to come and watch the drilling which would be conducted by Sergt Hook of Pershore. Instructions in signalling would be given by Mr Cholmondeley. Colonel Miller proposed a hearty vote of thanks to Mrs Smithett for coming and so closed the meeting.

MEMORIAL SERVICE AT THE ABBEY
Evesham Journal 10th February 1917

A memorial service was held at the Abbey Church on Sunday night for the 50 men fallen in the war who were residents of the ecclesiastical parishes of Pershore. The night was bitterly cold but the church was filled in every part, the congregation including the members of the Pershore Volunteer Training Corps under Commandant the Rev. H Clifford (who read the two lessons) and several of the parents and friends of the fallen soldiers. Many were unable to restrain their emotion when the names of their loved ones were read out and again when the solemn music of Chopin's Funeral March, beautifully played by Mrs Charles Mason, filled the sacred edifice. Two hymns were sung. 595 for absent friends "Holy Father in They Mercy" and 499 "On the resurrection morning". The Burial Service was read out by the Vicar who also preached a short but impressive sermon from the text found in the 15th chapter of the gospel according to St John, "Greater love hath no man than this that a many lay down his life for his friends.". He spoke of the many ways in which they could all honour the memory of the men who had sacrificed their lives for their country by thanking God for their bravery and devotion to duty, by living simpler and more godly lives, by showing self-sacrifice and practising economy, by placing their money, no matter how large of small the amount which could be spare, at the service of the country.

Berrow's Journal 5th November 1921
PERSHORE WAR MEMORIAL
Town's Proud Record

On Tuesday afternoon, Pershore's War Memorial in the Abbey Church was unveiled by the Lord Lieutenant (The Earl of Coventry) before a large congregation o the townspeople, relatives and ex-servicemen.

The memorial has been designed and sculptured by Mr Alfred Drury R.A. It consists of a winged figure of Immortality in bronze mounted on a Portland stone pedestal which bears the names of the men of Pershore who sacrificed their lives in the Great War. The figure of Immortality is represented as having alighted on the terrestrial sphere and is holding in her right hand the olive branch of peace while with her left hand she is seen bestowing "the Crown of Everlasting Life, the Crown of Glory that Ladeth not away". The winged figure, with flying drapery, gives an opportunity to the artist to make a rhythmic composition and to keep the figure in character with the religious atmosphere of the church.

The whole work is cast by the cire perdue (Wax lost) process which was employed by in his famous statue of "Perseus". This process ensures an absolute facsimile in bronze of the wax model as left by Benvenuto Cellini the sculptor's hands and the following inscription "To the Immortal Dead 1914-1918 Be thou faithful unto death and I will give thee a Crown of life". The memorial is certainly one of the most beautiful in the country and its setting in the south transept of the Abbey could not have been more fitting.

The unveiling ceremony was part of an impressive memorial service, conducted by the Vicar (Canon Stewart Robinson) and the Rev. J Dolphin. A procession was formed from St Andrew's Church to the Abbey Church and in this procession were representatives of every section of life in Pershore. The crucifer and acolytes, wreath bearer, bugler and choir led followed by the clergy of the Rural Deanery of Pershore (marshalled by the Rev H B S Fowler). There followed the Registrar of the Diocese (Mr W Stallard), Churchwardens of Holy Cross and St Andrew's, the Rev J Dolphin, the Rev. J B Hunt, the Rev Fr. Denys, the Rev H Clifford, the Vicar of Pershore (The Rev. Canon L S Robinson), the Lord Lieutenant of Worcestershire (the Earl of Coventry), General Sir Francis Davies (Scottish Command), Lt Colonel A H Hudson (Chairman Pershore War Memorial Committee), Mr J Willie Bund (Chairman Worcestershire County Council), Mr J Faulkner (Chairman Pershore District Council), Mr W J Gregson, Major W H Taylor, Major H Davies, Captain Elkington (Pershore Old Comrade's Association), Dr Emerson, Mr A W Smith (Hon Treasurer Pershore War Memorial Committee), Mr W J Gardner, C C, Mr W Wood (Chairman Pershore Board of Guardians), Mr W T Chapman (Chairman Holy Cross Parish Council), Mr T Gurat (Postmaster of Pershore), Police Inspector Grey, Mr H Bick (Chairman Ancient Order of Foresters), Mr J R Wilke (Chairman Independent Order of Oddfellows) Mr C Partridge (Chairman Cirencester Conservative Benefit Society) , Mr J R Coombe (Chairman Rational Mutual Benefit Society) and members of the Pershore War Memorial Committee. When the memorial had been unveiled, cadets bearing wreaths advanced and placed them in position.

LORD COVENTRY'S TRIBUTE

Lord Coventry said that he regarded it has a very high honour to be invited to unveil that memorial to the gallant men of Pershore who laid down their lives in the Great War. When recruiting commenced in the early days of the war, the men of South Worcestershire gave a hearty response to the call and Evesham, Pershore and Broadway would always be remembered for their ready and loyal response to the appeal. He was informed that the number of Pershore men serving at the time of the Armistice was 276; 89, alas, were killed in action, 12 died while serving and 27 were discharged making a total of 404. This was a record of which Pershore might well be proud. They must all feel that it was right and proper that they should place on record for all time the names of those valiant men who made the supreme sacrifice. They helped, by their bravery, to gain a glorious victory which they trusted might ultimately be the means of securing, with the blessing of God, peace and goodwill amongst all the nations of the earth.

"LEST WE FORGET"

The Rev. H Clifford said a dedicatory prayer and the procession returned to the Chancel. Speaking from the Chancel steps, General Sir Francis Davies, whose home is at Peopleton, said he had been asked to say a few words. He said they had come together on a very solemn and notable occasion. He ventured to say that such an occasion had never come about before in the long history of that ancient Abbey Church and he hoped the reason for it would never occur again. They had come together to do what little they could to honour the men of that town who gave their lives that they who remained might live and be free. Those men had brought them great honour: every one of those men had brought honour to his family and the town in which he lived. Nothing we could do could ever repay that debt. The Lord Lieutenant had told them how in the first days of the war, when the King's call came, the whole of the nation had rushed to arms and foremost among them were the men of their town. They bore themselves gallantly and every battalion of the County Regiment covered itself with glory. He hoped those things would never be forgotten. He asked those present not to think, when they had left the Church, that they had done all there was to be done in honour of those men. He would rather ask them to think that what they were doing that day was just the beginning of one long act of reverent remembrance and recognition of what those men had done. Let it not be said in years to come that it had been forgotten. He asked them to bring their children up in the understanding of what the memorial meant. If the child was a boy, perhaps the call might come in his time and he would do what these men had done. If it was a girl, they should remember the part that women played in the war. The girls should be told what the women of our generation did – how they sent their men to fight and never flinched, however great the sacrifice.

The names of the fallen were read out and the "Last Post" sounded. An offertory was taken for the memorial fund, the Committee of which are faced with a deficit of about £200. As the congregation filed past the memorial out of the church they reverently laid wreaths at the foot of it.

REMEMBER THE FALLEN WEBSITE:

If you are searching for information about Worcestershire men and women of both World Wars and the various wall memorials around the county, then we highly recommend that your first port of call is this brilliant website. Its creator, Sandra Taylor, has been of enormous support to us here in Pershore and we truly appreciate all her help and advice. You can visit her website at **http://www.rememberthefallen.co.uk** , find the memorial and then click on the name of the casualty.

Become a Friend of Remember The Fallen: In 2015, Lottery funding runs out and in order to keep this resource running, fund-raising will be required. One way you can donate is to become a Friend of the organisation. Please contact Sandra by email at tommy@rememberthefallen.co.uk or by post at Remember the Fallen, 3 Hunt Avenue, Worcester, WR4 0QW.

A visit of some of the Friends of Remember The Fallen to Pershore Abbey on Saturday 11th October 2014 greeted by Dr Judy Dale, Church Warden of Pershore Abbey and Mrs Trudy Burge, Hon Secretary of Pershore & District Royal Naval Association

WORLD WAR ONE 1914-18
How Worcestershire went to war

We are deeply indebted to Newsquest for their support and for allowing us to print the text of newspaper articles from local papers such as the Worcester Berrow's Journal and the Evesham Journal. As an organisation, they have fully embraced the Centenary of the First World War with marvellous features in their local papers and on their website and we continue to work with them closely. Visit their website http://www.worcesternews.co.uk for their WW1 feature.

They are appealing for any family memories or information on any of the Worcestershire men who served so please, if you have any information, contact them and hopefully they will cover the story. It's wonderful to learn about our ancestors locally and after all these years, it pays tribute to them all when they are remembered. Over the next 4 years, we plan to work together and publish articles on the Pershore Fallen as and when the Centenary Anniversary of their death comes round. Look out for them in the Evesham Journal or Worcester News. If you have any information on a relative, please contact them by telephone on 01905 748200 or via email:

peter.john@midlands.newsquest.co.uk
mike.pryce@midlands.newsquest.co.uk

EveshamJournal
http://www.eveshamjournal.co.uk/

Worcester News
http://www.worcesternews.co.uk/

Poem of Remembrance
By Bethany Ireland

The soldiers marched off one by one,
To do the job that had to be done,
'Your country needs you' the posters said,
But no one realised what lay ahead.

They gave their lives to protect us all,
With a willing heart they answered the call.
The battles raged and so many men fell,
Would anyone come home with tales to tell?

We must never forget the price they paid,
What selfless sacrifice the young men made.
As the years march silently by,
We must remember why they chose to die.

They fought for us so brave and true,
So let's all give them the thanks they are due.
And remember them as we silently pray,
That peace will descend on the world one day.

Winner of the Pershore Poppy Appeal Poetry Competition
2014 Bethany Ireland age 14 of Wick, Pershore
Student at Pershore High School